CAMP CADET

MENTORING AMERICA'S YOUTH

Evan K. Slaughenhoupt Jr.

ISBN 978-1-0980-5806-7 (paperback)
ISBN 978-1-0980-5808-1 (hardcover)
ISBN 978-1-0980-5809-8 (digital)

Christian Faith Publishing, Inc.
832 Park Avenue
Meadville, PA 16335
www.christianfaithpublishing.com

Printed in the United States of America

Matt,

Thank you so much
for the editing you
did that helped
produce this book,

fondly,

Evan K. Slaughenhoupt

24 NOV 2020   2/10

Camp Cadet Graduation at Camp Bucoco

DEDICATION

Mentoring America's Youth is dedicated to the men and women in law enforcement and nursing, in particular, the troopers, local police, nurses, and volunteers who voluntarily served their time to Camp Cadet.

It's said somewhere that the core values for law enforcement officials can be described using the acronym POLICE: professionalism, obligation, leadership, integrity, courage, and excellence. There are no more important qualities for law enforcement than honesty and integrity. Public trust of law enforcement is vital for individuals to have confidence in those granted such policing powers.

"Nurse: just another word to describe a person strong enough to tolerate anything and soft enough to understand anyone" (Author unknown).

"I attribute my success to this; I never gave nor took any excuse" (Florence Nightingale).

"The best way to find yourself is to lose yourself in the service of others" (Mahatma Ghandi).

"Nurses are there when the last breath is taken, and nurses are there when the first breath is taken. Although it is more enjoyable to celebrate the birth, it is just as important to comfort in death" (Christine Bell).

Three of the four original creators of Camp Cadet—Trooper (later Corporal) John J. Prandy, Trooper Robert W. Price, and Trooper Carl J. "Marty" Martynuska—are deceased as well as former Pennsylvania State Police Commissioner Colonel James D. Barger.

Commissioner Colonel James D. Barger

While commander of the Pennsylvania State Police Troop "D" when Camp Cadet was founded, then Captain James D. Barger advanced in his career becoming the Pennsylvania State Police Commissioner, overseeing the entire state police force. If it wasn't for James D. Barger, the Pennsylvania State Police Camp Cadet program would not be here today.

Born in Boston, Allegheny County, Pennsylvania, on May 16, 1920, he served as the state police commissioner from January 1973 to February 1977. Throughout his career, he was known to spend a good amount of weekend time visiting and inspecting troop headquarters and substations. Barger ordered the patrol car colors to be changed from blue and gold to blue and white color scheme. It was during Barger's tenure that the construction of the new state police headquarters located on Elmerton Avenue was started, though it was not occupied until his successor became commissioner.

Corporal John J. Prandy Jr.

The University of Indiana Pennsylvania created the John J. Prandy Memorial Award in recognition of the late Corporal John "Jack" Prandy, twenty-three-year veteran with the Pennsylvania State Police Force. The award is given to a criminology student who intends to pursue a career in law enforcement and presented at the graduation ceremonies in May. The award is based upon the student who best meets criteria as officially declared a major in criminology with a 3.0 grade point average and demonstrated involvement in community and/or campus activities, with preference given to those involving children and their welfare.

Corporal John "Jack" Prandy Jr., born June 15, 1942, passed away at age forty-six, on November 2, 1988, and is buried at Saint Bernard's Cemetery in Indiana, Pennsylvania.

Trooper Robert W. Price

Robert W. Price born August 2, 1937, in York, Pennsylvania, passed away at age eighty-one on November 10, 2018. Bob was a member of St. Ferdinand Catholic Church and a member of the

Cranberry Men's Club. He proudly served in the U.S. Marine Corps from 1955 to 1958. Bob retired from the Pennsylvania State Police and was a member of the Fraternal Order of Police, the U.S. Marine Corps League, and cofounder of the Pennsylvania State Police Camp Cadet program. Bob served on the Cranberry Township Board of Supervisors for seventeen years.

Trooper Carl J. "Marty" Martynuska

Carl J. "Marty" Martynuska was born July 1, 1940, in Lilly, Pennsylvania, and passed away January 7, 2020, at the Veteran's Administration Butler Healthcare Medical Center. Carl graduated from Cresson Joint High School then enlisting in the U.S. Army in 1961, where he served in the military police corps, until his discharge in 1963. He joined the Pennsylvania State Police and for years travelled with the state police rodeo. Until retiring in 1992, Carl assigned to the Butler barracks Troop D was a longtime leader of the Pennsylvania State Police Camp Cadet program for youths. He was well known as "Trooper Marty" while he served as safety education officer, visiting area schools. Carl was a member of American Legion Post 778 of Lyndora and the FOP Lodge of Meridian. Carl was an avid hunter, enjoyed watching Penn State football, and entertaining others with his unique sense of humor.

This book is also dedicated to one individual who was there at the beginning and remains so today "Nurse Nancy" Nancy Bard, wife of Trooper Paul Bard. Besides recruiting other nurses to participate, Nurse Nancy continues serving and, in 2019, received an award for fifty years of volunteer nursing work at Butler's Camp Cadet. The Camp Cadet program would not be the same except for her.

Nancy Bard received an award Friday, Aug. 9, 2019, for 50 years of volunteer nursing work at Butler's Camp Cadet.

"Nurse Nancy" Nancy Bard

Nancy also provided a list of nurses who served Camp Cadet Troop D in Butler:

Nancy Bard	Linda Campbell, CRNP
Debbie Bossinger	Sherry LeHere Puckett
Kathleen Brown	Emily Rekich
Rose Bush	Rose Szybka
Christle Callen	Jane Vasey

Rose Bush

Nurses were integral to the success of the Camp Cadet program. Rose Bush was recruited by "Nurse Nancy" Nancy Bard to participate in the camp. Rose Bush who was the wife of another trooper at the time and worked as a nurse at Butler Memorial Hospital. She volunteered her time to be a camp nurse and was very special to the camp program. Unfortunately, Rose passed away to cancer a few years into the program.

CONTENTS

FOREWORD

Colonel Robert Evanchick, named by Governor Tom Wolf as the acting commissioner of the Pennsylvania State Police effective March 24, 2018 and confirmed by the Pennsylvania Senate on June 4, 2019, says, "Since 1970, the Pennsylvania State Police Camp Cadet program has been an important part of the department's community outreach. The program, designed for boys and girls ages twelve to fifteen, is built upon the seven core values of our department: honor, service, integrity, respect, trust, courage, and duty.

Camp Cadet directors, staff, and volunteers are the living embodiment of those values, working year-round to plan and execute a series of camps throughout the commonwealth. More than a week in the summer for children to have fun, learn about law enforcement, and enjoy physical activity. The Camp Cadet experience also helps us bridge the gap between law enforcement and the public we serve. And the outreach works. In my time with the Pennsylvania State Police, I have encountered countless troopers who tell me they began thinking about a career in law enforcement after attending Camp Cadet as a teenager.

Over the past fifty years, Camp Cadet has been a source of pride for our department. The nature of policework means troopers regularly interact with the public in stressful, emergency, or other less-than-ideal situations. Camp Cadet gives its staff and volunteers a unique opportunity to slow down and make a real one-on-one difference in the lives of children.

The program would not be possible without the support of an extremely dedicated and committed group of people, and I thank everyone who has offered their time, expertise, or support to it throughout the years. The work you do matters, and the success of the program is reflected in each child who creates lifelong memories at Camp Cadet."

—Colonel Robert Evanchick

The author's accuracy in telling the story of the Pennsylvania State Police Camp Cadet program is spot on. He was there. He lived it, along with the cadets, the police officers, the nurses, the entire staff who made that initial dream come true. From the funny moments to the not-so-funny moments, he captured the essence of what it means to show young people how together, law enforcement and the youth of today, can succeed in attaining a mutual respect and trust for a voluntary compliance of the law.
—Albert R. Vish, Trooper (Retired)

ABSTRACT

For fifty years, the Camp Cadet program provides young people positive experiences with law enforcement for the primary purpose of improved community relations. It is only fitting that the Pennsylvania State Police receive recognition for creating Camp Cadet. In 2020, *Mentoring America's Youth* documents this successful program. Unique for its time, Camp Cadet was conceived to reach young people differently than previously done by law enforcement. This unique program continues within Butler County where it originated and expanded elsewhere throughout Pennsylvania as well as other states.

INTRODUCTION AND PURPOSE

Since 1970, a Pennsylvania State Police program called Camp Cadet brings youth together with law enforcement for the primary purpose of improved community relations. The goal was for youth to gain a better understanding of law enforcement through building a better relationship with youth. Such a successful program that expanded to other states deserves to be documented. For 50 years, Camp Cadet provided youth positive experiences with law enforcement. The reader will learn about the societal challenges that prompted creating Camp Cadet. Never previously reported insights are provided, as can only occur by those who began and sustained the program. The ups and downs and recollections are envisioned to encourage continuation of this program with a sincere outreach to the youth of America.

BACKGROUND
AND OVERVIEW

A criminal justice course called "Introduction to Law Enforcement," taught by Christopher Muscato who has a master's degree in history and teaches at the University of Northern Colorado, indicates a theory existed in the 1960s that police should be morally impartial. He also teaches how that theory changed during the 1970s by various police departments.

Christopher Muscato writes,

Policing in the 1960s

Police were supposed to simply uphold the law without getting personally attached to victims or suspects.

However, while the police wanted people to see them as an unmovable force of justice, the public saw something different. They saw police attacking peaceful civil rights protesters with hoses and dogs in Birmingham, Alabama, in 1963. They saw college students protesting war or racism shot by police in Jacksonville, Mississippi, in 1970, just after national guardsmen killed college students protesting at Kent State in Ohio.

The 1960s were a turbulent time when American society was full of protests about extremely sensitive issues and tensions were pretty

19

high. Police were not seen as impartial. Violent police actions damaged the reputation of police officers, greatly reducing the trust between police and citizens. Add in the assassinations of John F. Kennedy and Martin Luther King Jr., and you've got an era of absolute fear and little trust in the ability of the police to fix that.

Policing in the 1970s

After the traumatic 1960s, American police officers realized that some policies needed changing. As the sixties transitioned into the seventies, police departments focused on improving their images. Some efforts were successful, some weren't. One practice that made a big difference was the increase in *foot patrols*, officers who walked rather than drove around the city.

For decades, officers used their cars to demonstrate their impartiality, driving around to show their presence. Researchers of the 1970s found that this wasn't very effective but that foot patrols were. People wanted to get to know the officers; they felt safer when they saw officers walking around, and they felt like the officers; cared about their problems. Policing in the 1970s was characterized by a rise in community involvement as officers started trying to solve crime with the help of average community members. Still tensions were high after the 1960s, and in many places, this could escalate into violent altercations.[1]

---

[1] https://study.com/academy/lesson/us-policing-after-1960-influences-developments.html

Pennsylvania

In 1970, a unique effort was created in Butler, Pennsylvania. Three members of the Community Services Unit, Pennsylvania State Police Troop D, Butler, conceived, created, and developed a program called Camp Cadet. It was intended in part to help improve community relations between young people and the police.

The sole purpose of Camp Cadet was to change any perceived incorrect attitudes and images that young people might have had about law enforcement and the dedicated men and women who make up this necessary profession.

The thought was to change wrong attitudes and images by doing something with the young people and instilling in their minds that the police are truly interested in their well-being and not interested in arresting them.

Pittsburgh Press News Article

Impress Them Now or Arrest Them Later was the theme identified in 1972 in this special news article written by Robert Stearns.[2] In that article published after the third yearly Camp Cadet, an overview of the camp program is provided and sets the stage to learn details about how these troopers started the camp, the challenges they faced, how it became successful, and recollections by those involved.

"*We're* living in a society of gaps—a generation gap separating the young from the old. A credibility gap yawns between figures in high office and the voters who put them there."

But the gulf dividing policemen from the policed is being shortened somewhat through the efforts of a small group of state troopers stationed in Butler. For a week each summer, members of the State Police Troop D operate a boy's camp called Camp Cadet.

The purpose of the camp is to show young people that policemen are human, that they too can laugh and have a good time, and

---

[2] *Impress Them Now or Arrest Them Later*, The Pittsburgh Press Roto. September 17, 1972.

that cops are interested in kids' well-being and not just in arresting them.

"The answer to crime is not law enforcement but preventive education," said Maj. Michael Donahoe, director of the Community Services Bureau at State Police Regional (Department) Headquarters in Harrisburg. (The administration of the Pennsylvania State Police initially occurs at the department. It then branches out to "areas" and then "troops" then "stations.") "Our objective is to try and influence their sense of values. If we can convince them of society's need for rules and regulations, they will see the need for someone to enforce those rules and regulations."

Trooper Albert R. Vish

"We have to impress them now or arrest them later," said Trooper Albert R. Vish, community relations officer at Troop D. Vish. And two other troopers, Robert W. Price and John J. Prandy, dreamed up the idea of Camp Cadet two years ago. Since then, Prandy has advanced to corporal and other duties, and his spot has been filled by Carl Martynuska.

So dedicated to the concept of Camp Cadet is Prandy, this year, he offered to serve voluntarily. His offer was accepted gratefully by Vish, Price, and Martynuska, who need all the help they can get in riding heard on the fifty 12-to-15-year-old boys accepted for the week's encampment.

Camp Shaulis is the small area given over to the state police by Camp Lutherlyn, a church-operated camp near Prospect, in Butler County. "The boys are chosen on a first-come-first-served basis," Vish said. The first fifty who apply are the ones to go. "We have two pages of names of youngsters ready to step in if someone decides to drop out," Vish declared.

But there aren't any dropouts unless an emergency arises in the family or someone gets sick at the last minute.

A typical day at Camp Cadet starts with the flag-raising ceremony followed by physical training and breakfast. The rest of the morning is spent in classes: police history, traffic safety, studies on youth in trouble, FBI talks, first aid, and drug lectures. The afternoons are given over to recreation and free time.

Evening programs include guest speakers and films on such things as hunter safety, judo, and firearms. Lights out is at 10:30 p.m.

Starting from scratch two years ago, it was only natural that some mistakes would be made. "We're learning all the time," Vish admitted. "For example, we don't have field trips anymore. We used to take the kids on a trip to Moraine State Park, but that proved a real loser. To start with, they didn't like traveling in a school bus to get there. Then they said the boat ride was 'for kids' and the nature trail was 'for girls.' [Such were accepted attitudes in 1970 that would not likely be felt during 2020.] It's just as well—we have plenty for them to do right here."

There's a lot of marching and cadence counting at the camp somewhat reminiscent of marine boot training. Maj. Donahoe explained its significance.

"Marching teaches an understanding of discipline and discipline is the secret of success," said Donahoe, a veteran of twenty-six years with the state police. Speaking to the fifty campers, Donahoe said his hope was that they would learn self-discipline, he emphasized, there'd be no need for policemen.

While that need is sure to remain with us, you get the feeling in talking with men like Donahoe and Lt. John Angell, acting commander of Troop D, that they see each arrest as failure rather than a victory—a failure of society in implanting a sense of responsibility in the individual.

"Responsibility is the key word," Angell said. "We must teach our youngsters responsibility to school, community, country, parents, and self."

The week at Camp Cadet is free to the boys. The project, which costs about $2,500, is funded by service groups in Butler County. One anonymous donor, whose contact with the state police is through an attorney, has contributed $700 a year toward the operation of the camp. The troopers have no idea who the donor is, but this is one mystery they won't be investigating—they're happy to leave things just as they are.

"It costs $15 to $23 a day to keep a youngster in an institution," Donahoe said. "And while he's there, he doesn't get cured of his criminal tendency, he just becomes more proficient through association with experts. If this camp keeps just one kid out of such a place, it has paid for itself many times over."

The idea of Camp Cadet has been taken up by state police groups in four other areas: Erie County, Lancaster County, Chester County, and the State Police Academy at Hershey. "And there'll be more," predicted Donahoe.

The Erie program is funded through the county commissioners, who initially voted $1,500 to the project, Donahoe said. After the first camp, the commissioners were so impressed with the benefits, they upped their contribution to $5,000 so the program could be expanded to include more boys (and girls).

The state police places great emphasis on community relations. "Without the backing and support of the people, all is lost," Lieutenant Angell said. "How do we get citizen support? We have to earn it. We can't get it by putting an ad in the paper or merely by asking for it. We must get it by impressing upon the citizens the importance of their supporting good law enforcement.

"We have to show them what they stand to lose if crime and civil disorder are not curbed and what they have to gain if it is curbed. We get citizen support by instituting programs like Camp Cadet that will show our sincere desire to get involved not only with the adult citizen, but also with the young."

The message of Camp Cadet seems to be getting through. Many of the counselors who help the troopers run the place are former campers. One, on a two-week furlough from the Air Force, gave one of those weeks to the state police. He hopes to join the department after his military service.

Another expects to apply to the police academy when he's old enough. A third is enrolled in a college course in law enforcement with an eye to making that a career. These are side benefits, however. The really big objective is to change the attitude so many young people have about policemen. An indication of cadet's success is this comment from a fourteen-year-old camper:

> "I learned it takes more than a uniform to make a policeman. It takes a real man to be one. I don't call them pigs anymore."

PRE-CAMP CADET DAYS (EARLY 1970)

Much of this book relies upon the collaboration with Trooper Albert R. Vish. In an oral history interview in 2006[3] (adapted much throughout this book), Trooper Albert R. Vish reflects on the early days: "We had the basic safety education stuff in the schools, school bus safety, stranger safety, those kinds of things. But I don't think there was anything just geared toward young people in the sense of preventing crime. We were always investigating crime in an after-the-fact matter."

Looking back, Trooper Vish was somewhat correct in his assumption. Law enforcement was losing the battle and needed some way to prevent crime from happening in the first place. He and his two colleagues, Trooper Robert W. Price and Trooper John J. Prandy, were constantly talking and trying to develop new programs back then.

Trooper Vish says, "I don't know where I was when this thing hit me, maybe at home or in the office. But I started thinking if we could just show young people the other side of law enforcement and show them why we need laws—we need rules. I thought they would understand better the role and the function of law enforcement and people who enforce those laws and rules."

---

[3] Historical Memorial Center, Pennsylvania State Police, Oral History of: Albert R. Vish, June 12 and 13, 2006; Diaz Data Service, 331 Schuylkill Street, Harrisburg, PA 17110 (717) 233-6664.

One day in the office, Trooper Vish said to his colleagues, "Guys, listen to this. I got this hair-brained idea. I want to know what you think about it. I want to take fifty young men out to camp and spend a week with them and show them the other side of law enforcement. I want to show them that we truly care about their well-being. I want to show them that we're not just interested in kicking them off the street corners, harassing them and doing those kinds of things.

"They both looked at me and thought that I was nuts. After a while, it sunk in and we started bouncing this thing around, and they said, 'Al, if that's what you want to do, if that's your plan, we're behind you—we're with you.'"

Pictured standing from left to right is Trooper Prandy, Trooper Price, and Civilian Supporter. Seated are Captain Barger and Trooper Vish.

They had to sell the idea to the captain, and that wasn't going to be a soft sell. That was going to be a hard sell. The commanding officer was Capt. James D. Barger, but Al had an ace in the hole going for him. Al's relationship with Captain Barger was one anyone would be thrilled to have.

Trooper Vish says, "I can't say enough positive about the man. I think he was one of the best commanding officers I ever worked for and one of the best commissioners we ever had. He treated me like a son. There wasn't a thought that I could do wrong in this man's eyes, and he made me understand that and believe that—that's my ace in the hole."

When they went into the office and proposed this thing, Captain Barger looked at all three and said, "You know, Al, I think you guys are nuts, but you have my blessing and anything you need to make this program work. You come and see me, and it'll be done."

There was never a thing needed to make this program work that Captain Barger didn't supply. Trooper Vish says, "He was a strong trooper commander. He believed in the youth of Pennsylvania, and he believed in three young troopers at the time. If it wasn't for Captain (later Colonel) James D. Barger, the Pennsylvania State Police Camp Cadet program would not be here today. I never believed in my wildest dreams that Camp Cadet would still be here today."

It took about six to seven months getting the camp ready to begin in August. They had to come up with the programming, and funding was more of a challenge, so they split up the job. Trooper Price created the programming, and Corporal Prandy organized the funding while oversight of the entire project was done by Trooper Vish. It was very intense because naturally there were other duties to do. Fortunately, Colonel Barger (Captain at the time) gave his blessings, saying, "Go do what you have to do."

The funding back then was a challenge because Pennsylvania State Police policy would not permit any soliciting. They budgeted $3,000 to run the program. To raise that amount of money was made possible because the difference was Colonel Barger who was interested enough in the program; thought it was worthwhile and trusted the three to go out and solicit. Trooper Vish says, "How else could we come up with the funding? Nobody ever talked about it. Nobody questioned our motives. The three of us had our contacts and knew if we just talked about plans for the program, funding would occur."

Soliciting in uniform could be perceived as a problem if observed by someone not fully informed; specifically frowned upon. Trooper Vish says, "It's a no-no—not supposed to do that." However, if they were out doing a program somewhere such as the Kiwanis Club or Shrine Luncheon Club, they were in uniform. Low and behold, the audience would always ask about what they could do to help. Trooper Vish explained, "Well, amazing you would ask. We have this program called Pennsylvania State Police Camp Cadet, and it needs funds."

Ed Miller and Captain James D. Barger

As they began the planning, Mr. Ed Miller, who was the director of Camp Lutherlyn, was the first one approached for site location for the camp. While the church did not provide use of the camp for free, they did cut the cost to help keep within the $3,000 budget. That first camp for room and board cost $1,500. The remainder of the funds was used to acquire Camp Cadet T-shirts for the kids, sporting goods equipment and other expenses.

Trooper Price was working on the programming and conceived the camp being based upon a scaled-down version of the State Police Academy. In part, they wanted to instill traffic safety because these kids would soon become drivers. Trooper Vish says, "The age group of twelve to fifteen just sounded like a good age bracket to influence and impress them. Our own people, state troopers came in and taught these kids all about traffic safety."

To help advertise the program, they took advantage of their law enforcement positions as all had access to youths through the schools. Trooper Price was the safety education officer, Corporal Prandy, youth aid officer, and Trooper Vish was the community relations officer. Trooper Vish says, "Anytime we went to do a program in school, we gave our pitch for the State Police Camp Cadet program. That was an effective way to get the word out. A friendly local media also assisted with publicity. The problem was not getting the word out but devising a way to select the fifty campers because in 1970, we had over two hundred applications just for Butler County's first Camp Cadet."

They started selection on a first come, first serve basis. The first camp had fifty applications that came directly into the barracks, so those were the first fifty signed up for camp. The remaining 150 applications were put on an extra list. Of those first fifty applications, the troopers went out and interviewed each one individually; but only when at least one parent was present. They sat down and explained the program to each kid explaining what to expect, discipline, and schedule.

Trooper Vish says, "Discipline was paramount. It was number 1 for us." They demanded respect, received respect, and gave back respect to these kids. A key to success in the program is respect. During those interviews, they'd talk to the child more so than to the parent wanting him to know what he's getting into simply because the Pennsylvania State Police Camp Cadet program was not for everybody.

After about an hour of interview, Trooper Vish said, "The child was asked only one question: why do you want to go to this program? You can't look at Mom or Dad. Look at me and you tell me why you want to go." If their answer was, "Well, I really don't want to go, parents think it would be good to go," the child didn't go to the camp. It was essential the child wanted to go.

Camp Cadet was purposely intended to not solve discipline problems kids were having at home. While working on those types of issues discipline-wise, occurred at camp, the troopers didn't want to turn the program into another camp for bad kids.

This interview process worked well for a few years, but as the number of applications kept getting larger, another method was needed to select the campers. The county was divided into five sections and from each came ten kids. This provided a more cross-section representation from the county.

Given a camp of fifty kids, it seemed logical to divide into five parts with each group of ten having one counselor. Besides counselors, the staff included two nurses and the physical training instructor. Counselors were generally other law enforcement personnel.

The one individual who was there at the beginning and remains so today is "Nurse Nancy" Nancy Bard, wife of Trooper Paul Bard. Nancy in turn recruited other nurses to participate over time. Before the first camp, Nancy talked a nurse friend of hers, Rose Bush, who was the wife of another trooper at the time. Both Nancy and Rose worked as nurses at Butler Memorial Hospital. They volunteered their time to be camp nurses. They were very special to the camp program.

Camp Cadet was held at church Camp Lutherlyn who provided the cooks and maintenance staff. This permitted the number of Camp Cadet staff to remain small and effective. The initial idea was for all counselors to be law enforcement to include local police. Though other police officers were recruited, the need arose to extend the number of counselors to those outside of law enforcement. Everyone volunteered their time.

Trooper Vish said, "Nobody got paid, except we, troopers, who received our normal salary as this was simply another part of the job assignment."

THE FIRST
CAMP CADET

The first Camp Cadet was in 1970 with a program that is largely followed today. Camp began when the parents dropped off the boys at the local barracks in Butler. Campers were bused to the camp, and the first day was used to explain to them the schedule, rules, and expectations.

The mornings started at 6:00 a.m. with reveille, and "fall out for roll call" followed by physical training (PT). The PT instructor, Bill Schake, was not a police officer but a retired army paratrooper. Bill put them through their paces and expected a lot from them. He was a building contractor and just as tough as nails. The kids would fall out at six o'clock in the morning, and he would have them for about an hour.

During PT, the campers were learning how to march which instilled working together and discipline. Each morning included flag-raising ceremony to instill a sense of pride in our country. After PT, they would get cleaned up and ready for breakfast (8:00 to 9:00 a.m.) and then were in class from 9:00 a.m. until noon.

Classes consisted of Pennsylvania State Police history, the laws of the Commonwealth, driving, safety, and drug-related issues. They were shown how to take fingerprints and process a crime scene. The morning was mostly police-related classes.

Lunch was from noon to 1:00 p.m. Structured free time was from 1:00 until 4:00 p.m. Free time did not mean someone could just go off and do nothing. Trooper Vish says, "We had set up softball, volleyball, touch football, swimming, and such. But they were doing these activities with police officers." That was important for the kids to learn about the police officers being just regular people as the interaction brought emotional bonds.

This time also permitted the opportunity for a trooper or police officer to take a group of guys off in a corner someplace, sit with them, talk with them, answer any of their questions or concerns; answer questions about the job, what it's like being a policeman and such; all the while building trust and confidence in the developing relationship.

Original Camp Cadet Nurses Nancy Bard and Rose Bush

From 4:00 to 4:30 p.m. was a small break to get cleaned up and ready for dinner. Dinner was from 5:00 to 6:00 p.m., followed by a guest lecturer every night until 8:00 p.m. These sessions included someone from the FBI, classes such as two-day hunter safety course and first aid.

Free time from 8:00 to 10:00 p.m. was another opportunity for the campers to interact with police that included showing movies and question/answer sessions. Lights out occurred at 10:30 p.m., with the playing of Taps. Usually, the campers went right to sleep because 6:00 a.m. would occur very quickly to repeat the similar schedule.

Inspections Were Part of Camp Life

Following a weeklong camp (Sunday to Saturday), the end of camp was highlighted with the graduation. Though scheduled to start at ten o'clock in the morning, some parents were so excited, they arrived very early, as early as six o'clock in the morning. The graduation was very ceremonial and emotional as the pride those campers showed when they marched into the ceremony; for most the first time their parents saw them since Sunday. The transformation in just one week was a lifelong memory. As the ceremony ended, many were crying and wanted to stay an extra week; they just wanted to keep it going.

This daily schedule modified over the years but is still a core part of the daily program. Reflecting over the years about the first Camp Cadet, it couldn't have gone any better. It was the absolute best experience of his career. Trooper Vish said, "Camp was problem free, never wanted, nor needed anything. Everything that was intended for the camp occurred largely because of the support of Captain Barger. All the individuals presenting programs arrived on time. The kids were just absolutely a great bunch of kids. Though there was some homesickness, we handled the situation, and nobody went home. We never had any discipline problems. It was just a great and marvelous experience. Couldn't have been better. Everything went like clockwork."

For instance, Jon Iannotti, who attended the first Camp Cadet in 1970, is a managing member at USA Marketing & Development, LLC, vice president at Iannotti Realty Solutions, Inc., and former founder at FGCREIA (Florida Gulf Coast REIA). He graduated from Butler High School, studied criminology at Indiana University of Pennsylvania (IUP), and is currently living in Cape Coral, Florida, married to Stephanie Iannotti.

Jon Iannotti

Jon Iannotti says about the 1970 Camp Cadet, "Wow, this brings back memories. I was a Cadet at the 1st Camp Cadet! Went on to IUP Criminology, then hired as one of Cranberry Township's first Police Officers. Ended my career as chief of Buffalo Township (Sarver, PA). Could not have done it without the Camp Cadet Program!"

Captain James D. Barger, Troopers Vish, Price, and Prandy
Pennsylvania State Police Camp Cadet Graduation

The first camp was for boys only. Later, other camps were opened for young girls as well but not as coed camps. Female state troopers spearheaded the camps for the girls. Trooper Vish says, "We had boys' camps. We had girls' camps. They were separate to help keep the focus on the programs and learning discipline without the distractions from mixing the two."

Not being a camper himself, he once took a motorcycle trip to Canada and swore he'd never do it again. To this day, Al will tell you he is not a camper: "I'm people-oriented. I'm kid-oriented, but I've got to be inside. Got to have bathroom facilities indoors."

BUTLER COUNTY
CAMP YEARS

Troop D covered five counties: Armstrong, Butler, Beaver, Lawrence, and Mercer Counties. For a while, one camp was run in each county until those counties picked up on their own. Trooper Vish says, "We wanted them to develop their own programs to lessen any mixing of funding. We didn't want to take any boys from outside their home counties. This was to lessen the chance of someone saying, 'Hey, why do you have kids from outside of county when there's kids right here that want to go?'"

There were a couple of donors that took on the entire cost of the program for two or three years. The Shrine Luncheon Club aided greatly. Every year, they would provide between $700 and $1,000. No donor ever asked for any public recognition, but luncheons were held for these donors. "We'd bring them out to camp. They loved sitting there speaking with the campers."

Typically, on Wednesday during camp, the State Police helicopter would fly in for a visit. The donors along with the campers enjoyed watching it land. Camp Cadet remains blessed with all donations, but particularly the donors during that time.

Second Camp Cadet, Camp Counselors, 1971

At the Lutherlyn camp, there was a lake where the kids could go swimming. The lake had fish that the campers were able to catch. The facility was large enough to host multiple camps at the same time without any mixing or interfering among the various camps. Besides an ongoing band camp, Camp Cadet was provided a separate campsite such that nobody bothered Camp Cadet. There were about fifteen small cabins in a circle that housed ten kids apiece. Each had their own showers. Trooper Vish says, "Camp Cadet had its own parade field; all and all a very nice arrangement. Camp Lutherlyn was home for about the first ten years or so. It did start to get a little pricey, so we looked for another location."

Camp Cadets Listen Intently

Relocated to a Boy Scout Camp, Camp Bucoco in Slippery Rock worked well as they also had an outdoor swimming pool, but the cabins were more rustic as the boy scouts were accustomed to more roughing it than typical church camp attendees. With Camp Bucoco, the Camp Cadet program was able to stay within the $3,000 budget. In these early years, expenses never exceeded $5,000 to $6,000.

Camp Cadet nurses Nancy Bard "Nurse Nancy" and Rose Bush became part of the family. Unfortunately, Rose passed away to cancer a few years into the program, but Nurse Nancy is still involved to this day. She also goes often to Hershey, Pennsylvania, for the Commissioner's Honor Camp.

Standing Left to Right, Counselor Evan K. Slaughenhoupt Jr.,
"Nurse Nancy" Nancy Bard. Kneeling Left to Right Trooper
Carl L. "Marty" Martynuska, Trooper Albert R. Vish

Nurse Nancy is the longest serving Camp Cadet person and
the only remaining one active since the very first camp. The fondest
memory about Nurse Nancy is there was not one graduation in all
those years that she didn't cry. Each staff person was encouraged to
stand at graduation and share their thoughts and feelings with the
parents. Trooper Vish learned to automatically take out a hankie or
a box of Kleenex and put it at the podium. Nurse Nancy always
expressed the most heartfelt feelings about the campers and her being
part of Camp Cadet remains truly treasured.

The camp always had on staff at least two nurses. They were
qualified and legally, the only ones allowed to give out medication.
Upon arrival at camp, all medication were turned into the nurses'
station to ensure proper amounts were provided at the proper time.
They had a big responsibility and never faltered, never wavered.

Nancy Bard, Christle Callen, Kathleen Brown

Early years when the campers were dropped off by their
parents at the barracks included a class photo

Troopers, Staff and Counselors (1971, Camp Cadet)

CADETS' REUNION — Alumni of State Police Camp Cadet, held for the past two summers at Camp Lutherlyn, attended a reunion party and fun day yesterday at the Butler Cubs ASA Hall, the former YMCA on South McKean Street. More than 100 youths who had attended the camp sessions were present for the party, swimming period and games. Greeting the youths are, from left: Anthony J. Zaccari, Cubs president; Troopers Albert Vish and Robert Price, from the State Police; and "Dutch" Dorcy, city fireman and Cubs member .

Camp Cadet Reunion Reported in Butler Eagle

Camp Cadet Counselor Howard Johnson says, "I met Al Vish for the first time as a Camp Cadet counselor in 1973, in Butler, Pennsylvania. I was a criminology major in my junior year at Indiana University Pennsylvania. I was encouraged to participate in Camp Cadet by my role model, Trooper Pete Marsico, a Marine and Pennsylvania State Trooper. Pete served many summers with Al in the Camp Cadet program. Al headed up the program that summer. He went out of his way to make me feel welcomed, and I never forgot that. My life goal was to become a Pennsylvania State Trooper. I did not get into the state police but did serve as a Cranberry Township Policeman in the years following college during the late 1970s. I later became a science teacher and had two awesome students who were brothers, Mike and Matt Carcella, both now living the dream as Pennsylvania State Police Troopers."

Trooper Vish tells a story about how one year, on a Friday evening in preparation for the upcoming Saturday graduation (Camp ran from Sunday to Saturday) where typically a party was given to the campers, an issue arose about food.

Trooper Vish says, "Sometimes, a band could be arranged for the campers' entertainment, but a pizza party was the anticipated minimum expectation. One camp did not have any cooks available for that week. A dear local police officer Sergeant Gary West 'Sarge' of the Butler City Police said, 'Al, don't worry about it. I'll take care of the kitchen and the cooks for this program.'"

"How are you going to do that?"

"Well, I have some friends at a nearby installation. They have kitchen facilities. They have cooks. I'll go over there and see if I can talk them into coming up to cook for us."

For that week, as everyone arrived for camp, "Here comes Sergeant West, and he's got two individuals in tow. They're in uniform carrying their bags and were introduced as working at a local nearby installation."

Al thought, *Oh, great. Okay. We're in good shape. They're going to cook for fifty kids, staff of ten. It's not a problem. We, he can handle it. Right? Well, I knew we had a problem.*

During the week, Sergeant West was seldom seen as he spent all his time in the kitchen with the cooks, making sure everything went well. Throughout that week, one cook would go to Sarge with every problem. Sergeant West was "in charge" of the kitchen.

Toward the end of each day, the staff gathered to discuss the day and plan for the next, go over any issues or problems that needed to be addressed, "The first evening in walks this cook, in his uniform, looking good. Well, he's carrying a cookbook. I knew we had a problem from the beginning when I saw that cookbook."

The situation wasn't known how bad it was until a later staff meeting when the discussion turned to the planned Friday evening party. Having cooked all week, the cooks were just plain tired. The plan was to have pizzas delivered uncooked and then cooked on site. The cook, very tired, said, "Sarge, I understand we're getting like thirty or forty pizzas for the kids tonight plus a lot of 'Corn on the Cob.' How am I supposed to cook this pizza, you know it's the end of the week?"

A breaking point had been reached, and Sergeant West snapped at the cook saying, "Cook them in the box." Sergeant West was obviously kidding, but by the end of the week, he had just about enough with these cooks and never thought in his wildest dreams the instructions would be taken seriously.

Six o'clock that evening, several camp staff went down to the kitchen, and there was a smell. The cook literally did as he was told and put the boxes in the oven. "Sergeant West just went bananas."

The rest of camp staff were howling with laughter. "Thank God several went there to check when they did or that place would have burnt to the ground. It worked out though as the pizzas were removed from the boxes, put on trays, and were cooked perfectly."

As with all camps, winning the trust and admiration of those young campers really made some positive impact on crime. "That's where it needs to start, with the kids, young kids. They need to learn that somebody cares about them. In fact, the Pennsylvania State Police Camp Cadet program is the best community relations program going."

Another Camp Cadet. Another Camp Cadet Graduation.

Discipline was a key to the camp's success. Mostly for minor offenses, a couple of push-ups were needed while at times running laps seemed more appropriate. At times, the entire ten-boy squad was punished, not just the individual boy. They needed to learn that camp was a cooperative effort and what one does can affect others. What happens to one happens to all; working together as a team was critical. If one was caught doing something they should not be doing, the entire squad could be doing pushups or laps or even kitchen duty such as cleaning up after the meal.

The camp was specifically not intended as a "bad kid" camp. During the interview conversations, nobody was specifically asked if they ever had a run-in with the law. However, the camp did have some campers with some history. For example, the Juvenile Probation Office in Butler County asked if they could send five kids who were on juvenile probation. They were accepted and attended.

Counselor Russ Benninger (standing far left) and Campers in their 10 Person Squad. Russ became a Pennsylvania State Trooper and is now retired.

If a kid cared enough and really wanted to go to camp, they went. During the early years of camp in Butler, it was possible some of the campers did later run askew of the law. The Camp Cadet program didn't track them to measure success. One-week camp influence yielding perfect citizens who never created crime was not the objective. Trooper Vish says, "Life is life, and while some may have become a challenge, several, perhaps a dozen or so, did go on to become local police officers while yet another dozen went on to become Pennsylvania State Troopers or other forms of law enforcement, though that was never the intent of the program."

Camp Cadet played its role of influencing the opinion citizens had of law enforcement. In the 1960s, young people just did not approach police officers. They would speak when spoken to, but then a big swing in attitude was noted by police officers. Kids no longer appeared to fear approaching a police officer. They learned the main job of police is not to kick them off the streets, not sit around in donut shops but rather help citizens solve problems.

Trooper Vish tells how rewarding it is to have a former Camp Cadet camper approach and say how much they remember the camp and the great time they had. Many wanted to attend more than once, but attendance was limited to just once.

Camp Cadet expanded to include a camp for girls around 1973 when the first females were graduating from the Pennsylvania State Police Academy. Two troopers were assigned to Troop D: Trooper Marilyn (Reber) Stackhouse and Trooper Kathryn (Hosmer) Doutt. Assigned to community relations, Trooper Doutt helped with the boys' week one year and then with encouragement decided to put on a girls' camp separately.

Left to Right: Troopers, Vish, Prandy, Martynuska, Doutt, and Price

Camp Cadet worked well for the girls. They deserved and received everything the boys did and had just as much fun at camp. The programming was changed a little, tailored to the physical and emotional differences between boys and girls. That difference played a big factor in having separate camps instead of imposing coed camps.

Following high school graduation from Iroquois Area High School, Erie, Pennsylvania Trooper Kathryn (Hosmer) Doutt went to St. Olaf College, Northfield, Minnesota, before attending the Pennsylvania State Police Academy in Hershey. She also excelled in various traffic institute and leadership training throughout her career and a multitude of professional training opportunities.

Trooper Kathryn (Hosmer) Doutt, advanced in her career becoming a corporal from 1980 to 1986 and sergeant from 1986 to 1988 in the planning and programming in the Bureau of Research and Development. In 1988 to 1990 she was promoted to lieutenant overseeing Patrol Section Commander & Station Commander then captain as Troop Commanding Office & Internal Affairs in 1990 to 1995, finally to major as director, Bureau of Patrol 1995 to 2004.

Major Doutt, now retired, reflects upon those early days,[4] "Women did not become a part of the Pennsylvania State Police (PSP) until 1972. I was assigned to the Community Services Unit at Troop D, Butler, in July of 1972. Shortly thereafter, since my coach was Trooper Al Vish, I was assigned to help with Camp Cadet. That way, the boys could see that women were now an integral part of the PSP.

Captain Kathryn Doutt

---

[4] *Kathy (Hosmer) Doutt's Notes and Reflections on Camp Cadet*: February 24, 2020

"The first girls' Camp Cadet was actually held in Erie County sponsored by PSP Troop 'E' (much to my dismay). I was assigned to be one of the leaders at that camp.

"I think that the Butler County Girls' Camp Cadet may have started in 1974. I know that in 1975, both Butler and Beaver Counties of Troop D had girls' camps. In fact, Beaver had a girls' camp and no boys' camp. At 7:00 a.m., reveille sounded, followed by exercise and/or a run. Mornings were filled with educational sessions—at least twenty of them. Topics ranged from 'Women in the State Police,' 'Drug and Alcohol Use,' 'Hunter Safety,' 'Baby Sitting Safety,' 'Criminal Investigation Procedures,' 'Fingerprinting,' 'The Court System,' 'Traffic and Bike Safety,' etc. Volleyball, canoeing, swimming, and softball were held in the afternoon, weather permitting. Evenings often included special demonstrations and presentations, such as martial arts by a police instructor, police canines, etc. Each cabin had a counselor, usually a college student or a teacher.

"Originally, the Butler County Girls' Camp was led by me, Trooper Marilyn (Reber) Stackhouse, and a teacher from the area. Troopers Vish and Martynuska also made appearances. Other women Troopers, e.g. Jill Bairhalter and Jean Keller, also helped at various camps. The Beaver County Camp was led by Trooper Bill Morrison and me, with assistance from an area teacher and college students, the latter being counselors. Instructors were specialists in their field and included FBI agents, county judges, local and state police.

"There was always an invitation to the respective county children's service and/or probation office for recommendations, which also allowed for a broad spectrum of backgrounds into the mix. In addition to the applications, each girl was interviewed to ensure their interest in the camp and not that they were being pressured by their parents or others to attend.

"As stated already, the funding came from nonprofit organizations, but it also came from companies and industries who believed in both law enforcement and in youth. Beaver County's first camp was also partially funded by a grant from the Governor's Justice Council.

"Starting the girls' camp(s) in Troop D was a challenge. Since few thought women were on the state police, young women and girls didn't have as much interest in a camp structured by law enforcement to teach law enforcement-related subjects. Even finding women to help in leading and being counselors was not an easy task. I was not from the Butler area, so I did not have a ready-made group of women friends or acquaintances to ask. Female troopers were few and far between. For one camp, a trooper from Troop E, Erie, came to help; for another year, a trooper from Troop A, Greensburg, was assigned; and another trooper came all the way from Troop F, Montoursville, to assist. When another trooper was assigned to Troop D, she also helped in leading the camp.

"As with the boys, the girls learned that not all troopers are alike, just as they were not all alike. Parents of both boys and girls who had attended camp would come up and tell us how amazed they were at their children's changed attitudes when they came home from camp. They would actually make their beds, say please and thank you, and have a *ma'am* or *sir* mixed in their conversation. What a difference a week made!

"My eternal gratitude goes Trooper Vish, who always had faith in me; to the parents who entrusted their children to our care; to the children who actually wanted to come and experience interaction with law enforcement and learn about our responsibilities and duties; to the volunteers who actually made it possible; and to those who funded the camps."

Albert Vish is state trooper of the year

A former Sewickley man has been named State Policeman of the Year. Albert R. Vish, who served on the Sewickley Police Department prior to joining the State Troopers in September, 1967, was given the award at a luncheon meeting of the Pennsylvania District Exchange Clubs meeting at Seven Springs, Pa., on June 30.

Trooper Vish is assigned to Pennsylvania State Police Troop "D" in Butler, Pa., at the present time.

The award was given as an acknowledgement of his success in establishing rapport between the State Police and the young people of the Commonwealth. He accomplished this by instituting a Cadet Camp in Butler County, a week long summer program for fifty boys. Begun in 1970, it provides an opportunity for boys to associate with law enforcement officers in an informal setting and gives them an insight into the duties of a state policeman. Boys enrolled in the program range from 12 to 15 years of age. The objective of Trooper Vish's camp was to imbue the youths with a healthy respect for themselves, the rights of others and an orderly society. A cross section of the whole community is selected for camp attendance.

Trooper Vish's example and success in planning, organizing and fund raising on off-duty hours has been adopted in other areas in the Commonwealth.

Albert R. Vish

Trooper Vish is married to the former Norma McMillen of Leetsdale. The Vishes have three children, Carrie, Robin and Albert.

Attending the luncheon at Seven Springs when Albert Vish received his award were his parents Mr. and Mrs. Ted Vish of 728 Washington Street, Sewickley. Other members of the family and friends attending were: Mr. Dom Vish, his brother, Mrs. Leo DeGori, his aunt, Mr. and Mrs. Mike Settembrine and Mr. and Mrs. Albert

In 1973, Trooper Vish was awarded the Trooper of the Year as an acknowledgment of his success in establishing rapport between the state police and young people of the Commonwealth of Pennsylvania. Captain Barger had nominated him for the award given by the Exchange Clubs of Pennsylvania.

Over the years, situations did occur at various camps. There were a couple of broken arms. One young man fell out of a tree that he was climbing although was told numerous times not to climb the trees. Other situations were minor as well such as one having their hand slammed in a screen door, a broken finger but nothing major.

Trooper Vish was petrified of the lake and boating activities as he was not a water person comfortable in that environment. He says a big fear was having a staff member say, "Al, we can't find so and so."

Trooper Al Vish and Slippery Rock College Lt. Tom Reese

Animals were a source of contention as Trooper Vish hated bats and Trooper "Marty" was petrified of snakes. Morning before reveille, Trooper Vish typically stood on the camp staff cabin porch so the campers would see he was already up before them.

A Courageous Trooper Marty Touching a Snake

Trooper Vish recalls, "One morning while standing on the porch, there was a big pole holding up the roof. While leaning on the wall in my shorts, in my Camp Cadet staff shirt looking good, I looked over, and on that pole, fellow staff who were up before me caught a live bat placed in a cage and tacked the cage to that darn pole.

"I'm standing there, and I turn around and look at that bat and I, oh my. I went crazy. I screamed. Others, who were hiding behind the building, were howling with laughter. I jumped up. My feet never left the ground until I was out on the road which was about fifty yards down the end of the yard. Those guys thought it was just hilarious. The next day I got up, they had my underwear up the flagpole."

CAMP CADET ORGANIZERS — Displaying the Camp Cadet pamphlets and T-shirts are, from left: Lt. Arnold Fonseca, commander of the staff services section; Tpr. Carl Martynuska, safety education officer; Tpr. Albert Vish, community affairs officer; and David Say, Jaycees representative in charge of fund raising. Fifty Butler County boys will be selected to attend this summer's camp session at Camp Bucoco.   — PSP photo

Command and community support—vital as depicted in this 1977 news article

While Trooper "Marty" was fearful of snakes, Trooper Vish was not so afraid but said he really didn't like them in his bed like the time he recalls a chilly of kind at night. "I had a light overhead that I used to read he was lying there in his bunk and looked up and. Wrapped around my light is a snake."

Camp shenanigans were not just directed toward Trooper Vish who says, "We got Sergeant West one day. We tacked his entire sleeping bag, sandals, and shoes to the ceiling. It was so funny. It was a good time. I miss it very much."

It wasn't always camp shenanigans; sometimes, some time-out or direct counseling was needed for the campers. Once, one camper just seemed to have some difficulties or at least some different goals in mind. To help make the proper mental adjustment, a long walk was initiated which included a very heart to heart conversation. The never to be named camper did make significant improvements. Of course, such an exercise by a counselor one-on-one needed to be briefed to the troopers as depicted in this local *Butler Eagle* newspaper article and photo.

Counselor "Briefing" Trooper at Camp Bucoco

The newspaper reported, "Evan K. Slaughenhoupt Jr., chief of staff at last week's Pennsylvania State Police Camp Cadet program, and Trooper Albert R. Vish, co-camp director for the program, discuss some of the daily activities planned for the cadets." What the newspaper photographer reporter did not hear was that the briefing included the comment, "Al, I walked that young camper all the way here to get his attention."

The kids always kept staff on their toes. Trooper Vish recalls standing at the staff cabin looking out at all the cabins during clean up time before lunch. He saw a squad of kids across the field standing outside their cabin waiting for the last kid to join them so they can go to lunch. When he came out, they all turned around for some reason. Suddenly, all nine campers were howling with laughter as the tenth one showed up and had his shorts down around his ankles. Some of the campers had run up and pulled down his shorts.

While the shorts around the ankle could be just kids being kids, remembering the discipline being instilled could have probably been the cause. These campers were ensuring another in their squad would not make them late for lunch—self-discipline at its best.

At times, there were various field trips. During one trip to Slippery Rock Creek for a canoe trip, it started to rain. Getting off the creek as quickly as they could to get the campers back to camp meant pulling off in a little opening of the creek. As it just so happened, the location was an individual's backyard who wasn't happy receiving visitors. The property owner came down screaming, asking why they were there. At that point, many campers became muddy from falling into the mud trying to get the canoes out of the creek.

The angry guy threatened that he was going to call the police on everyone until he was told, "We are the police." He then calmed down, and everyone made it back to Camp Cadet with all needing to take showers. The experience caused some rethinking whether field trips should occur; particularly after another trip included paths and trails to see blazing flowers that may be unique to Butler County, but flower watching was not in the interest of the young boy campers.

Young boy campers were more interested in learning gun safety and shooting guns. Some classes included learning about black powder, flintlocks, and that some of those guns were made in Pennsylvania. There were two gentlemen, Trooper Paul Bard (Nurse Nancy's husband) and Charlie Walksmith who taught the classes and gave the demonstrations. Each camper had the opportunity to fire one of the flintlocks; some perhaps the only time they would ever fire a flintlock.

Camp Cadet Schedule for 1974.

Butler Eagle News Articles

A fifth camp in 1974, reported locally in part as, "Building boys' bodies and minds has been the goal of the five-year-old Camp Cadet program. (Trooper Al Vish's) principal assistants this year were Troopers Carl Martynuska and Donald Checkan. 'These men don't act like police officers,' said young David Pizer of Maria Lane, Zelienople, one of the camp attendees.

"All eyes of campers and many of their parents, who came to visit, were turned skyward Wednesday afternoon, when State Police Commissioner Colonel James Barger 'dropped' down on the camp via helicopter to pay his annual visit.

"Although this year's camp was the fifth year since it was founded, six camps have been held, an extra one in 1971, making a total of three hundred boys attending so far at Camp Lutherlyn.

"Helping in special presentations were members of the FBI, Don Martin of the State Game Commission, Roger Latham, Pittsburgh Press outdoors writer and others.

"Offering their services as camp nurses were two of the wives of state troopers, Mrs. Paul Bard (Nancy) and Mrs. Rose Bush along with Mrs. Jane Vasey, an area resident."[5]

Works in Background Trooper 'Marty' Makes Camp Cadet Meaningful, written by John R. Buchter[6], says about Marty:

"The objectives of an entire program are seldom reflected in the work of one person, but at Lutherlyn last week, Camp Cadet and Carl Martynuska were synonymous."

"Trooper Marty" who was attending his third state-police-sponsored camp goes about the business of gaining the confidence and admiration of young people with a quiet determination. His subdued manner often leaves him in the background, but the success of his efforts stands out in the minds of his coworkers.

---

[5] "State Police Hold Fifth Cadet Camp at Lutherlyn," Butler County News, *Butler Eagle*, Wednesday, August 28, 1974, page 8.

[6] *Butler Eagle*, Monday August 26, 1974, page 36.

Trooper Albert Vish, originator of the camp, emphasized Marty's importance, commenting, "It's Carl that makes Camp Cadet run." Vish explained that Trooper Martynuska is responsible for the programming and scheduling at the weeklong camp.

A Challenge

Marty, a ten-year state policeman who serves as the Youth Aid officer for the five-county Troop "D" area, looks on the business of planning the camp, not so much of a task as a challenge to make the boys "pull together as a unit and learn."

Involvement is Trooper Marty's key at the state police camp as he attempts to establish programs that are not only interesting but meaningful.

The programs include self-defense, first aid, hunter safety and youth counseling sessions with representatives from Children's Services and Butler County Juvenile Division.

It is the counseling area in which Marty excels. As Trooper Vish explained, "Carl gets wrapped up in kids and takes their problem and makes them his. Outside of Carl's wife, Kay, I probably know him best, and I know he really goes all out for the kids."

Carl's youth-oriented attitude is apparent in his reaction to a question on what is needed at the camp. He explained he would like to see the session expanded to two weeks with the possible addition of a week's program for girls.

The major stumbling block in expanding the program, Carl said, is the cost of the operation. It currently costs $3,000 for the sponsorship of the one-week outing. The money pays for the lodging and meals for the fifty boys.

Personalities

One of the more interesting features of Camp Cadet belongs to two men most responsible for its operation. The almost paradoxical personalities of Vish and Martynuska are described in their own words as: "The Screamer vs. The Teddy Bear."

Instead of clashing with one another, both men agree their conflicting personalities seem to broaden the Camp Cadet experience and enhance their personal friendship.

Marty explained, in somewhat of an understatement, "Al expresses himself more, but we tend to have the same ideas and thought." Vish said, "I have a hard line, but Marty soothes things and makes things work."

The complementary personalities appear to have worked quite well, for this is the fifth year for Camp Cadet.

CAMP CADET SCHEDULE

AUGUST-74	18-SUN	19-MON	20-TUE	21-WED	22-THUR	23-FRI	24-SAT
6:45 A.M.		FIRST CALL	←				→
7:00-7:15		FLAG RAISING	←				→
7:15-7:45		PHYSICAL TRAINING	←				→
8:00-8:45		BREAKFAST	←				→
8:45-9:00		CLEAN UP	←				→
9:00-9:50		PSP HISTORY	FIRE PREVENTION	SCUBA DIVING	FIRST AID	← →		INSPECTION
10:00-10:50		FLAG RESPECT	YOUTH PROBLEMS	↑	NARCOTICS PROGRAM	RADAR DEMO	GRADUATION CEREMONIES
11:00-11:50		F.B.I. AGENT	SECRET SERVICE	TRAFFIC SAFETY	↓	↓	
12:00-1:00		LUNCH	←				→
1:00-4:30	ARRIVE AT CAMP	SPORTS FREE	←				→
4:30-5:00	PHYSICAL EXAM	CLEAN UP	←				→
5:00-6:00	SUPPER	←					→
6:00-6:45	SKYDIVERS	FREE	←				→
6:45-7:00	SPORTS AND FILMS	FLAG LOWERING	←				→
7:00-9:00	↓	SOFTBALL GAME	HUNTER SAFETY	← →		GUN EXHIBITION	ROGER LATHAM
9:00-10:00	TAPS	←					→

Camp Cadet Schedule for 1974

Other Staff

The third cog in the state police camp team is Trooper Donald Checkan, safety officer in his first year.

The camp counselors include: Evan K. Slaughenhoupt Jr., formerly of Butler, who is an Air Force sergeant at the National Security

Agency; Don Lee, a master's degree candidate in Criminology at Indiana (Pennsylvania) University; Henry "Chip" Christy, also an IUP grad student in criminology; Rick McKnight, a Butler County Community College student and a former Camp Cadet enrollee; and Dennis Dague, a respiratory therapist at a Pittsburgh area hospital.

A class speaker was identified who spoke at graduation and was selected by his fellow campers. Graduation activities at Camp Cadet concluded Saturday with the awarding of the Colonel James D. Barger Award to the outstanding cadets in the age groups represented at the camp. A special award, a baseball autographed by Willie Stargell, was also given to one of the boys.

Class Speaker Albert T. Vish, selected by fellow campers. Proud father seated to the right in background.

To earn the Colonel James D. Barger Award required nothing phenomenal. The camper had to demonstrate participation, leadership qualities, and was split into the various age ranges. Selection was done by the camp staff counselors who really appreciated being part of the decision-making process. The troopers were not involved in the decision as to ensure no bias should some of the campers' parents be state troopers. The James D. Barger Award was a prized item for the campers. In 1976, it was awarded to Carrie Ann Vish for Outstanding Thirteen-Year-Old.

At times, funding permitted the creation of a "Camp Cadet Memory Book." Though professionally done, they were expensive to produce.

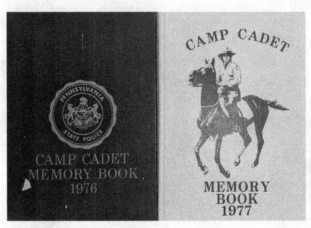

Camp Cadet Memory Book

One year, Trooper "Marty" took over the programming inheriting the responsibility to ensure that programs ran on time. Whoever was supposed to speak had to be at camp on time for Marty to show them where they had to go, get them to the classroom, and other logistics. One day, Marty was very uptight over the program involving a young lady from Juvenile Probation, Children's Services.

The lady was supposed to come in and tell the kids how easily they could get into trouble, not by doing anything wrong but just being in the wrong place at the wrong time. Marty was so uptight because his first program presenter was late, the second one never showed, and this lady was to be the third one.

She was five minutes late getting to the campsite. Several of the staff met her at the entrance to the camp, knowing Marty was on edge. The group talked her into just leaving her car there. Taking out a map, she was given instructions to walk down the road where Marty was standing and nervously awaiting her.

Marty was a total wreck. Al tells us, "She takes this road map, and she's walking down this path toward Martynuska, and she's looking on the map trying to find some point of reference, but there wasn't any. She's in the woods for gosh sakes. She looked like she was lost. She was totally lost reading that roadmap. Marty saw her as the rest of us were hiding in the woods laughing.

"Marty was so upset, and when he saw her never said hello to her, turned around, walked into the classroom, and never said anything. We finally had to get her and bring her to the classroom and introduce her. We never let Marty live down as to how 'had' he was by us."

Activities provided a great way for the campers to interact with law enforcement and staff.

'MOM' THROWS PITCH — Butler Memorial Hospital nurse Nancy "Mom" Bard hurls a pitch during an afternoon softball game at the Pennsylvania State Police, Camp Cadet for boys. Bard, who's been with the camp since it began, says she wouldn't think to do anything else during Camp Cadet week. The program borrows 50 boys for a week and shows them that policemen are people too.   — Butler Eagle photo

While the *Butler Eagle* newspaper provided a wonderful image of such activities, here is what the pitch looked like that Nurse Nancy threw to the batter.

CAMP YEARS
THROUGHOUT PENNSYLVANIA

As Camp Cadet started small, nobody would have believed it would grow, but it did; and over time, more structured policies and organizational constraints became inevitable. For the first ten years, there was no board of directors. It was just a few troopers putting on a camp. No one envisioned the potential growth. Then command changes started influencing the program.

Authorities in Harrisburg were getting more involved because the Bureau of Community Services wanted to know what the troopers were doing out there with the camp. The legal department started to get involved as well. Soon, directives started flowing such as identifying the need to establish a board of directors. The troopers were instructed to "run the camp" and let the board raise funding. So Camp Cadet needed to become a nonprofit organization and established a 501(c)(3).

Permission was needed from Harrisburg for various items such as using the Pennsylvania State Seal and calling the program the Pennsylvania State Police Camp Cadet Program.

As part of fund raising, Trooper Vish had one idea that was quickly dismissed. He wanted to "auction off a trooper for a day." The idea was a donation would provide a trooper to do whatever they wanted for a day, for instance drive around, take them to a store, do their shopping, or clean their house. The captain distinctly said, "Al, you're killing me." So the fundraising resorted to more traditional bake sales and dances.

By 2006, the number of camps like Camp Cadet increased even into other states, Trooper Vish recalled being set up and ready to attend one held by the Kentucky State Police but, for some reason, was unable to attend.

Troop D Commanding Officer, Captain Steve J. Ignatz

Just following his February 21, 2020, input to this book, Captain Steve J. Ignatz was promoted to major and began his new assignment as executive director of the state police Municipal Police Officers' Education and Training Commission in Harrisburg, Pennsylvania.

Now Major Steve J. Ignatz says, "My earliest memory of the state police was as a young boy growing up in Leechburg, Armstrong County. Several of us were outside playing when I saw a marked state police car drive down Pitt Street. I remember seeing the big antenna swaying back and forth when the trooper parked the car and got out. He was at least eight inches tall and looked impressive in that gray uniform. From that moment on, I wanted to know what the state police was all about. A few years went by, and I had seen state troopers in my school giving their safety speeches from time to time. I was always impressed by the troopers, the way they conducted themselves, and that gray uniform.

"At some point in school, it was announced that the state police was hosting a summer program called Camp Cadet. It was going to be held at the Sky Meadows Girl Scout Camp near Avonmore in Armstrong County. I remember being very excited about the prospect of attending such a camp. My parents were enthusiastic about the camp, and we got an application sent in right away. I remember the excitement I felt when the word came that I had been accepted to the camp. Two other boys in my neighborhood were also going, so it was going to be great. We had to go to the state police barracks near Kittanning for an interview. It seemed like a big trip for me, but it was only twenty-five minutes from home. Trooper Jacob Zellie oversaw Camp Cadet, and he seemed like he was 'all business.' I remember him giving a little overview of the week and what was expected. He told us about the campsite being somewhat primitive and we would be expected to get up early and do dishes. My mother wanted to know if I should get a tetanus shot before camp started. The rest was a blur. When we left the barracks, I remember my dad saying that Trooper Zellie must be a marine. How he knew that or why he thought that, I do not know. My dad was an army veteran, and he always held marines in high esteem and often remarked to my brothers and me about how tough marines were. I think he also wanted me to think it was going to be a rough week.

"The week of Camp Cadet came. We were assigned to one of several cabins around the Girl Scout Camp. I did not know anyone assigned to my cabin. We again got to see Trooper Zellie as well as several troopers who were helping with Camp Cadet throughout the week. One of the troopers, Al Vish, would have a lasting impact on me. He was the trooper who came up with the idea for Camp Cadet, and through his fostering, the program spread across Pennsylvania and into other states to be adopted by other State Police/Highway Patrol agencies. He was kind and caring and very funny, at least I thought so. I remember him playing a tiny harmonica during the week. I would ask him years later about the harmonica. He still had it and was surprised I remembered such a thing.

"In addition to troopers assigned to Camp Cadet, we also had civilian counselors. These men were good-natured people who wanted the 'cadets' to have a fun time during our stay. Trooper Zellie would carry a big walking stick when he would march or run the cadets (which seemed like constantly!). One of the civilian counselors took our squad for a hike and got lost. We ended up several miles from camp and only could get back once we hit a main road. Clearly, this was a learning experience for everyone involved since this was the first Camp Cadet in Armstrong County.

"During the week, we got to see firefighters, police officers, emergency equipment, and other things troopers work with every day. The troopers were certainly enjoying themselves too. They would ride between the cabins using the red lights and sirens on their cars. They would broadcast silly things over the public address systems. They would tell stories and jokes at night. At one point, the cadets were lined up and we were marched through teargas. I cannot imagine that happening today! This was the best summer event I had ever attended!

"As near as I can recall, the first Armstrong County Camp Cadet was held in 1975. I say 'as near as' because no one remembers the year for sure. I had a graduation certificate, but it was lost years ago. I have known the counselors for many years and have worked with Camp Cadet since 1993, yet the date continues to elude us. I still have my Camp Cadet shirt that was given for the graduation ceremony. While my friends who attended Camp Cadet wore their shirts all summer long and to school the following year, I did not want mine to get worn. I proudly kept it hidden away in my dresser as I grew up and throughout my adult life. I love to take it to the Camp Cadet graduation exercises when I am asked to speak.

"I knew from seeing the state trooper on my street in the late 1960s that I wanted to wear that gray uniform someday. Camp Cadet sealed the deal. Cadets got to see troopers as they really were, not robots along the highway passing out speeding tickets. They were people who enjoyed having fun. They cared about the kids in their care and worked extremely hard to make sure we all had a fun time. I wanted to be a part of that. Giving young people a little glance behind the curtain of law enforcement was not only eye-opening for me, but it lit a fire that has never gone out. I got my first job in law enforcement at nineteen years of age. I worked for two municipalities until I was hired by the Pennsylvania State Police. I have now worked for the PSP for thirty-five years and have enjoyed it every day.

"I have been friends with the original Camp Cadet counselors for many years. We still get together and help at the Armstrong County Camp Cadet. Camp Cadet has evolved over the years and now includes girls and boys. It still provides the kids with a week of great fun and adventure as well as a way to see law enforcement.

"I have told Trooper Vish, now retired, that I owe my career with the state police to him and Camp Cadet. It is true. As an impressionable kid, I could have easily gone down another path—good or bad. Camp Cadet taught me much in one short week. Much of what I did that week, I remember to this day. Camp Cadet was new and developing when I was given the opportunity to attend. Interacting with the troopers for the week has led to a career, family, and lifelong friends. Trooper Vish could not have expected his vision would be so profound. From the bottom of my heart, I thank Trooper Vish and all who have worked so hard to make Camp Cadet what it is today."

Darlene Geibel of Saxonburg, Pennsylvania, writes: "Our family's connection with the PA State Police Camp Cadet Program in Butler County began in 1974 when my sister filled out an application and was accepted at the age of thirteen. Fast-forward ten years and our son and two of my nephews put in their applications and were accepted that same year to the Butler County/Troop D Camp Cadet program held at Camp Bucoco Boy Scout Camp near Slippery Rock, Pennsylvania. My one nephew was also chosen to give the graduation speech that year. It would be another nine years, and two more nephews would attend Camp Cadet (they are brothers of the nephews who attended in 1984), and the one nephew that year was also chosen as the 'Outstanding Cadet.'

"Little did we know these first encounters of family members with the Camp Cadet program and again over the next few years with our son becoming more acquainted with Trooper Al Vish through our church would set into motion a connection with the PA State Police and the Camp Cadet program that would continue for many years to come.

Ronald Geibel, Retired Captain Dan Hines, Darlene Geibel

"Fast-forward and in 1998, after seeing an article about the PA State Police accepting applications for the academy in Hershey, I wrote our son, Dan Hines, who was serving in the army as a military policeman. He still had the memories of the Camp Cadet program and the desire instilled by Trooper Al Vish to become a trooper himself. That dream came true in March 2000 at his graduation from the PA State Police Academy in Hershey.

"It would be another eight years, and our oldest granddaughter would attend the Armstrong County Camp Cadet program and was chosen to represent her class as the Honors Cadet at their graduation and to also attend the 2009 Pennsylvania State Police Commissioner's

Honor Camp at the State Police Academy in Hershey. But the connection doesn't end there. Our son's daughter applied and was accepted into Troop D's Camp Cadet program in 2017 and again in 2018 as a Phase II counselor. We can proudly say, our family's history and connection with the PA State Police and the Camp Cadet Program has spanned several generations and over forty years, and we can affectionately say, "We owe it all to Al Vish. Thank you, Al!"

Retired Captain Dan Hines, now working at the Denver, Colorado District Attorney's Office, says, "Al and I met at St. Paul's Catholic Church, where he as a Eucharistic Minister and I was an altar boy. My World War II grandfather (Pap) had just been diagnosed with brain cancer and died shortly after I attended Camp Cadet. Pap was my hero, so it hit me like a ton of bricks. Al became that role model and filled the void. I wanted to enlist in the army because of my pap. I wanted to enlist in the state police because of Al Vish. There are countless stories like mine. He's an amazing man."

From Left to Right, Sydney Hines (Daughter),
Taryn Heines (Wife), Landon Hines (Son), Captain Dan Hines,
Darlene Geibel (Mother), Ron Geibel (Father)

Dan further says to Trooper Vish, "I want to publicly thank you for the inspiration and example provided to me all these years. Although many know you as Retired Trooper Al Vish, the man who started Camp Cadet, I first got to know you from church in Butler, Pennsylvania. A few years later, as a young child attending the Pennsylvania State Police Camp Cadet program, I honestly thought you were seven feet tall, and there was a cape waving in the wind behind you. I would have never imagined I would someday wear that same uniform and all my dreams would eventually come true. I never really got to thank you for such a wonderful career filled with a wide spectrum of emotions and memories. My children, who are now teenagers, have only known the life of being the child of a state trooper. As such, they understand sacrifice, and they respect our true heroes. The support my wife Taryn Hines provided throughout my career enabled me to follow my careers dreams wherever they took me. I had the opportunity to work throughout Pennsylvania. I was blessed to have worked with some of the most amazing troopers and staff members. In the later part of my career, I was continually amazed to just step back and really appreciate the dedication and commitment. My own professional commitments carried me throughout Pennsylvania and out to numerous states, to include New Jersey, West Virginia, Washington, DC, South Carolina, Virginia, New York, Ohio, North Carolina, Maryland, Delaware, Colorado, and Kentucky.

"Most importantly, some of my proudest moments involved the chance to impact other young children in several Camp Cadet programs throughout Pennsylvania. I shared the same beliefs with people like Joseph Nolte, Bob Bemis, Juliet Nolte, Julie Montgomery, Robin Freeman, Amy Santelli, and many others. I was fortunate enough to also witness my niece and daughter graduate from Camp Cadet.

"Now as reflect back on my journey, a simple 'thank you' seems so insignificant to the man who provided me with the catalyst to make it all happen."

Trooper Richard Reitz, retired, started the Camp Cadet, in Troop F, Lycoming County. He says of Trooper Al Vish, "I always admired the way Al Vish is recognized as the 'Father of Camp Cadet' in Pennsylvania with the Pennsylvania State Police."

Trooper Richard Reitz

"In January of 1975, as a trooper with the Pennsylvania State Police serving as a Troop Youth Aid Officer with in a nine-county area of Pennsylvania, I was dispatched to Syracuse University to attend a conference addressing the problems with youth of America. At that time, there was not a good relationship with young people and the police departments across the country. Police departments from various cities and states across America were invited to this conference. After numerous workshops with the young boys and girls, it became obvious that various problems regarding arrest procedures and investigations with youth had to be addressed. At the same time, the youth and their parents had to know what law enforcement responsibilities were and how the laws were enforced.

"After the conference, I made a report of my interpretations of what the conference offered to the Lycoming Brotherhood National Conference of Christians who paid for the trip to the university. The brotherhood invited me to sit on their board to which I accepted.

"My commanding officer, Captain David C. Martin, invited me to his office to discuss the results of Syracuse conference. He informed me that he had attended a conference with all sixteen troop commanders in the state at State Police Headquarters in Harrisburg,

Col Barger, the commissioner of the Pennsylvania State Police informed all the commanders that they should make an effort into establishing a Camp Cadet program in each of the sixteen troops in the state. Captain Martin instructed me to find a place where we could start a program and instructed me to visit Butler County Camp Cadet in the Western part of the state.

"That same week, I drove to Butler County to observe the State Camp Cadet program in session at the time. I met Trooper Albert Vish who was there as camp director. He showed me the curriculum and the fifty boys who were going to different scheduled events. I asked Al about various items such as implementation of funding, how the cadets were selected, and what age groups were at the camp. Trooper Vish gave me various forms showing scheduling, interviews, and what cadets needed to bring to their camp. After a two-hour visit, Captain Martin called me and asked me to come back to our troop headquarters at Montoursville, Pennsylvania. Thus, I thanked Trooper Vish and drove back home.

"The next day, I drove to a campsite in the northern part of Lycoming County along Pennsylvania Route 14 called Camp Susque. After meeting the camp director, Mr. Ditmar, and informing him what my intentions were, he agreed to rent the campsite for boys for one week in June and the other week in August for girls. I informed him that I would have to find funding and get back to him.

"At the board meeting for the brotherhood, I asked for help to fund the program. Mr. William Pickelner, president of the brotherhood, advised me that they would set up a committee to help fund the program. Trooper John Madey, the community relations officer of Troop F, and I went out to various organizations and contacted various community leaders. Those entities agreed to work with Mr. Pickelner and his committee.

"Each school district was notified about formation of the Camp Cadet program, and each principal agreed and would allow us to interview various candidates after they filled out an application to attend. Interviews were conducted in each of the seven school districts in Lycoming County. Trooper Madey and I then selected fifty boys to attend in June and fifty girls to attend in August. We set the age groups of students at twelve to fifteen.

"Scheduling was addressed following Trooper Vish's format, and all different law enforcement agencies were invited. The mission of the program was designed to bring a better understanding between the youth and its law enforcement officials. The goal of the program is to provide a weeklong experience for boys and girls that will be remembered by all cadets who attend and to create that lasting impression that police officer are their friends.

"The 'memorable experience' at Camp Susque will provide a setting that provides plenty of outdoor activities. As programs for competitive participation in canoeing, BMX bicycling, riflery, archery, mini motor bikes, and a variety of team sports such as softball and volleyball.

"The camp also provided the atmosphere of a police academy. Emphasis is placed on self-discipline to encourage some form of regimentation in the campers' personal live. The cadets were divided into for different groups or companies in each of the three campsites at Susque. This camp is beautiful as the settings of mountains in the background along with the Lycoming Creek bordering the campsite. Big open fields with a pond, a swimming pool, and shower rooms gave good access for programs of scuba diving, swimming, and canoeing.

"The first day of camp finally started Sunday, June 13, 1976, and fifty boys appeared along with their parents on Sunday. Parents were invited to attend visitation night on the Wednesday of that week and to pick their child up on Saturday morning at 10:00 a.m. after graduation exercises. Besides serving as a counselor, two other troopers from the patrol division also served as counselors, Trooper Martin and Trooper Slocum, were assigned to companies. Mr. Larry Strausser, a law enforcement professor at Lycoming College, and Mr. James Smith, a fitness and first aid instructor, were invited to serve as counselors. A local resident, Nancy Ludwig of a neighboring village (Trout Run, Pennsylvania), was invited to be the camp nurse. I served as camp director.

"Graduation day came on the Saturday after a good week with the boys enjoying a Friday night celebration party doing skits while eating pizza at a camp fire. Captain David Martin assigned his traffic lieutenant to inspect the cadets after they marched into the flagpole facing their parents. An 'open ranks' inspection was held as the lieutenant marched through stopping at times to talk with several of the cadets. The cadets responded 'yes, sir' and were dismissed after receiving their diplomas.

"The staff and I cleaned up and inspected all the cabins and tents. I thanked the staff and went home exhausted but can only thank Trooper Vish because this program would never have been started except for him and Col. Barger.

"In August of 1976, on a very hot day, fifty girls arrived at Camp Susque. We had no female troopers in Troop F. I think that the first female troopers graduated in 1975 and there were only a few at different stations throughout the Commonwealth. I invited schoolteachers, Juvenile Probation officers, and Children & Youth Case workers to assist as counselors. I do not remember their names. I really believe that as being one of the first cadet programs we were the first class to graduate fifty young girls. Captain David C. Martin attended this program and inspected the girls after marching into the flagpole facing their parents.

"Since then, approximately four thousand youths have graduated from our program. Three other programs were started in the Seven County Troop F area. The program was restructured in 1979, and it is currently operated through the combined efforts of all law enforcement agencies in Lycoming County. In 1986, Camp Cadet became an incorporation with the board of directors assuming the responsibility for the program's operation.

"After nineteen years at Camp Susque, the board of directors decided to change the site of the Camp Cadet program to Little League International Little League World Series grounds in South Williamsport, Pennsylvania, where we can house boy and girls in the large dormitory buildings. I retired in 1991 but stayed on the board of directors and served to assist the camp director as a consultant and camp counselor.

"At Little League, we have almost all the services as we did at Camp Susque, a large cafeteria, a recreational building, sixteen dormitories to house the one hundred cadets. We changed the curriculum a bit and interfaced some actual police oriented which cadets participate such as tactics and criminal investigation. The Game Commission comes with a live bear which they put to temporary sleep and pull a tooth. The Fish and Boat Commission also come along with the FBI and Arson Investigators. The Pennsylvania State Police Helicopter arrives as it did at Camp Susque and the Life Flite Helicopter arrives from Geisinger Hospital. Other presentations include Emergency Services Ambulances, Fire Engines, and a live Police Stop demonstrating a K-9 apprehension.

"At Little League graduation ceremony, the parents arrive on Friday night to observe the girls and boys march to Volunteer Stadium as their parents watch in the stands. We lowered the age for cadets to attend at twelve and thirteen to reduce possible intimidation by older youths. We also eliminated parent visitations to reduce the chance of homesickness.

"In closing, I sincerely thank Trooper Albert Vish for his vision as well as Colonel Barger (deceased) as this program now encompasses twenty-seven other areas in the state. Each year, two top cadets from each program are invited to the Pennsylvania State Police Commissioner's Honors Camp at the Police Academy in Hershey, Pennsylvania. Many of the graduates have become Police Officers with the state, city, and local departments. In our program, we have three graduates of West Point. I still attend every year and hope to make the fiftieth anniversary.

Shawn Widenhofer, class of 1983, and son Seth Widenhofer, class of 2019, say the following: "Camp Cadet is an institution that has withstood the test of time." Both Shawn and Seth learned core principles of discipline, honor, self-esteem, and teamwork.

Seth Widenhofer, Al Vish, Shawn Widenhofer, 2019

They say, "Discipline plays an important role in Camp Cadet activities. The early morning physical training and the regimented schedule helps to instill a discipline and work ethic in the youth that most have not experienced. This discipline and work ethic that begins the moment they arrive for registration, continues at a high level until after graduation ceremony has concluded. Being told where to go and what to do helps the cadets realize that time is valuable, and a lot can be accomplished if time is spent the right way."

Shawn Widenhofer and Parents, 1983

"Cadets are taught to honor the United States of America, Camp Cadet, and themselves. Honoring the United States of America and the flag is one of the very first lessons at camp. Understanding and honoring the flag as well as what has been sacrificed to enjoy the freedoms that we have today is conveyed to the cadets.

"Conducting oneself in an honorable way and with high integrity is expected to maintain the honor of both the participant and Camp Cadet.

"Self-esteem is taught in various ways at Camp Cadet. Cadets learn to overcome obstacles and are encouraged to push past the doubts they have and ultimately succeed. Even just choosing to attend this camp and completing it instills self-esteem that the cadets will carry with them forever.

"While attending Camp Cadet, teamwork plays a pivotal role in developing relationships with peers and staff. Learning to work as a team to overcome obstacles that one could not overcome alone is a very rewarding experience for both the staff and participants. The volunteer staff is firm and fair when encouraging students to push through the hard times and persevere, both as an individual and as a team member."

Shawn saw his son Seth complete the first year of the program and noticed the same rock-solid foundation that he experienced thirty-six years earlier. "Built on top of that foundation are more period specific adaptations to topics of today. As the cadets focus on the founding principles for a week, the cadets get a new appreciation for the troopers, their parents, and themselves. Trooper Vish was truly a visionary in starting this camp and helping it grow across Pennsylvania.

"The dedication of the troopers, volunteers, and sponsors should not go unnoticed. Without them demonstrating discipline and teamwork, none of this would be possible for the youth."

More recently, Camp Cadet in Butler County moved back to Camp Lutherlyn from Camp Bucoco. The program changed over the years too in some respects. The kids are supplied much more such as uniforms whereas the early years was just a T-shirt that said Pennsylvania State Police Camp Cadet. The campers wore shorts mostly, but that T-shirt was provided for their graduation so when their parents saw them for the first time since going to camp, the T-shirt was the uniform.

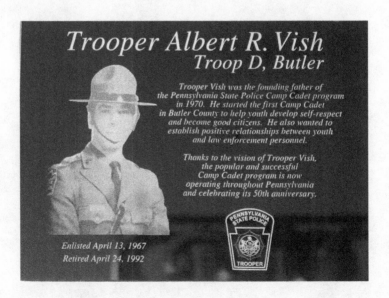

Trooper Albert R. Vish
Troop D, Butler

Trooper Vish was the founding father of the Pennsylvania State Police Camp Cadet program in 1970. He started the first Camp Cadet in Butler County to help youth develop self-respect and become good citizens. He also wanted to establish positive relationships between youth and law enforcement personnel.

Thanks to the vision of Trooper Vish, the popular and successful Camp Cadet program is now operating throughout Pennsylvania and celebrating its 50th anniversary.

Enlisted April 13, 1967
Retired April 24, 1992

Trooper Albert R. Vish retired April 24, 1992, after twenty-five years and spent several years conceiving a means to document the memories of the Camp Cadet program. His contributions to this book highlighted a career of contributions to society and the well-being of fellow citizens. From being named Trooper of the Year in 1973, to being honored with the invitation for participating in an oral history program in 2006, to a plaque presented at the State Police Academy in 2019. The plaque was presented to Al Vish by Camp Cadet Butler, with a second plaque sent to the State Police Historical Museum, at the State Police Academy, Hershey, Pennsylvania. A most humble person, like many heroes of the past, Trooper Albert R. Vish is truly treasured by many who know him and had the privilege of working with him.

Corporal David Jungling, Pennsylvania State Police presenting
Al Vish with the plaque for starting Camp Cadet fifty years ago.

Camp Cadet and similar programs this camp inspired remain active today. Camp Cadet Troop D now has a presence in social media such as their page on Facebook. The social media tool demonstrated a means of reconnecting former campers. Westmoreland County, Pennsylvania, also has a Camp Cadet and a presence on Facebook.

Trooper Dan Kesten, director of the current Butler Camp Cadet

Trooper Kesten says, "Trooper Michael V. Markey and I became the codirectors of the Troop D Camp Cadet in June 2007. I had never been involved or had any knowledge of any Camp Cadet program before this time. Therefore, I relied heavily on Trooper Markey, who attended the 2006 Troop D Camp Cadet as a staff member, and Mrs. Nancy Bard, who had been at every Troop D Camp Cadet since its creation in 1970. Of course, others provided input as well.

"We were in a tough situation as the organization didn't have enough money to conduct the camp in the upcoming August as scheduled. Trooper Markey and I hit the streets seeking donations. The response from businesses, community groups, and individuals was terrific, and the organization soon had plenty of money to conduct the camp.

"We had a meeting with a retired marine corps drill instructor named Carl Curtis. Carl had a great deal of successful youth mentoring experience. He agreed to help us plan for the upcoming camp and run the physical training and drill and ceremony portions of the camp. His top Ambridge JROTC Cadets were eager to spend the week helping as well. He was also instrumental in bringing a high level of discipline and regimentation to the camp.

"So we were all set, and when August 2007 came, we got our start with just over forty kids. We, of course, had a lot of assistance from the nurses, troopers, and civilian volunteers. We had a couple of cadets from the 2006 camp on hand to assist as well. A great team is what we ended up with. That team allowed for a very successful camp.

"Trooper Markey and I decided to increase the numbers of campers and ramp up fundraising for the following years. With the help of the board members, we were able to soon have a secure financial future and ended up with over one hundred kids at the camp in just several years. Recruitment efforts were paying off as we began to see more and more applications each year. Trooper Markey and I decided to allow any past graduate of the program to return as a junior counsellor if they desired. Soon, we were swamped with kids wanting to return.

"Trooper Markey left the program after four years with his acceptance of a promotion to corporal. I credit him as the driving force for the success that the camp achieved for the kids. In 2014, due to being overwhelmed with returning graduates as junior counsellors, Anthony Tripp and Kaleb Martin, who were long time volunteers at the camp as Ambridge High School JROTC Cadets, developed and ran the Phase II program named the Camp Cadet Leadership Development Program (CCLD).

"In 2015, Major Christopher Augustine (retired U.S. Army, Special Forces, and current Perry High School JROTC instructor) joined the CCLD team and took the CCLD program over in 2018. Due to many of the CCLD Cadets wanting to return to the camp, in 2015, two fifteen-year-olds, Emily Kesten and Gavin Terwilliger, developed and ran the Phase III program named the Principles in Practice Program (PIP). These additional programs were developed to satisfy the implementation of Corporal Markey's rule of never telling a kid that he or she cannot attend the camp.

"In the following years, the team had great success. In 2016, Trooper Josh Black and Trooper James Long joined the team and really added great insight. Trooper Black went the extra mile ensuring that the financial security of the program will last for many years.

They each were instrumental in the redevelopment of the camp to provide a fresh new camp once again. The new version launched in 2019 focused more on smaller groups within the camp spending more time with their police officer squad leader. The kids still, however, take part in physical fitness activities, drill and ceremony, and platoon games. Of course, the law enforcement classes remain intact as well.

"In 2019, Troopers Long and Black became codirectors who implemented great ideas. In 2019, the range was eliminated and replaced with paintball which the kids really enjoy. I expect to continue as a codirector for several more years and hope to see the camp continue along the same path of our great team of volunteers, board members, and nurses constantly generating and implementing new ideas and strategies.

"Troop D Camp Cadet offers a unique opportunity for youths to build moral characters and develop strong leadership traits. The foundation of the program is discipline and regimentation as we recognize the importance of these factors and their benefit to an individual and society. The goal of Troop D Camp Cadet is to introduce participants to the diverse criminal justice system and establish a positive relationship with law enforcement personnel. Camp Cadet is structured upon training at the police academy. Cadets are required to participate in all scheduled events and quitting the camp is not an option. The camp focuses on discipline, self-esteem, teamwork, drug and alcohol education, violence prevention, and many other issues facing today's youth.

"When asked how Troop D Camp Cadet benefits a child, I tell them: Troop D Camp Cadet is conducted in an atmosphere of discipline and regimentation. The child will learn how to apply these standards to his or her life. They will also learn or build upon their existing self-discipline, respect, self-respect, patriotism, honor, teamwork, leadership, and other character traits which are essential for life success. It is our goal to provide all cadets with the tools to develop them into the most honorable citizens with the ability to lead others while building a strong relationship with law enforcement officers."

Information regarding the three phases:

Phase 1 (Basic). For youths twelve to fifteen who never attended Camp Cadet.

Phase 2 (CCLD—Camp Cadet Leadership Development). For graduates of Phase 1 and those over fifteen years of age who have not attended Phase 1.

Phase 3 (PIP—Principals in Practice). For graduates of CCLD.

Phase 1

Who can apply for Phase 1?
Youths of good character who will be between the ages of twelve to fifteen on the first day of camp and reside in Butler, Beaver, Mercer, and Lawrence Counties can apply.

What will I experience as a Cadet?
You will embark on a life-changing experience through discipline and regimentation realizing that everything in life is possible. There are fun activities and police demonstrations as well. The six-day/five-night camp is modeled after the Pennsylvania State Police Academy. You will be challenged mentally and physically on your way to achieving success while gaining unwavering self-confidence and determination. Strong bonds will be built between you and your classmates and your law enforcement leaders as you endure the challenges, have fun, and achieve success as a team relying on one another.

What a day is like at Troop D Camp Cadet?
Camp Cadet is "basic training" for citizens of good character. The "basics" demand a sense of responsibility and respect. The days begin with wake up at 5:00 a.m., and cadets are in formation for physical training by 5:15 a.m. sharp. Reveille and flag-raising occurs after breakfast. Flag-lowering is at sunset, with lights out at 10:00 p.m. A rigid schedule of events will influence the activities during

the week. Cadets will function as a unit; they sleep, eat, march, learn, and play together. The two platoons compete against each other in physical contests throughout the week. Camp is not all work; however, each day includes ample recreation time and law enforcement and character development classes as well.

Who is Troop D Camp Cadet best suited?

Troop D Camp Cadet is for youths who are interested in a challenge and building a strong moral character or who have an interest in law enforcement or military careers.

Phase 2

Who can apply for CCLD (Phase 2)?

Graduates of the Troop D Camp Cadet Phase 1 program who are under eighteen years old and who continue to live by the standards of Troop D Camp Cadet are eligible to apply. In addition to these applicants, any youth of good character who did not attend Phase 1 but is between the ages of fifteen to seventeen on the first day of camp can apply. However, preference will be given to past graduates.

What will I learn at CCLD?

CCLD, or Camp Cadet Leadership Development, is an extension of learning of the Phase 1 program. CCLD Cadets will undergo intense leadership training. You will learn personal development techniques to mold a strong moral character making you fit to become a sound leader. You will also be provided with training giving you a base of knowledge and skill to lead others in a positive direction in an effective manner.

What is CCLD like?

The same standards are expected of each CCLD Cadet as are expected of the Phase 1 Cadets. CCLD Cadets are expected to arrive standing tall and looking sharp on day one to pick up right where they left off after Phase 1. It is expected that each CCLD Cadet conduct himself or herself with the highest standards of honor and self-discipline without the instructors having to "reteach" these traits. You will eat and do PT with the Phase 1 Cadets. You will sometimes act as instructors and leaders for the Phase 1 Cadets by attending some of their competitions, drill practice, and other activities. CCLD Cadets will also be taking part in their own intense training of leadership education separate from the other phases at the camp. If you did not attend Phase 1, don't worry, we will get you up to speed.

Phase 3

Who can apply for PIP (Phase 3)?

Graduates of the Troop D Camp Cadet CCLD (Phase 2) program who are under eighteen years old and who continue to live by the standards of Troop D Camp Cadet are eligible to apply. Participation in Phase 3 requires a previous or future commitment to year-round activities which benefit Troop D Camp Cadet and the applicant. These activities include fundraising, Phase 1 recruiting, and/or public awareness presentations.

What will I learn at PIP?

PIP is an extension of learning of the Phase 1 and CCLD programs as well as an opportunity to put your learning into real-world practice gaining valuable education, experience, and contacts. PIP Cadets will undergo success and motivation training teaching you how to apply your Camp Cadet skills outside of camp. You will continue to learn personal development techniques to mold a strong moral character making you fit to become successful. Some skills that you will learn are job-seeking and interview skills, courtesy, fundraising, public speaking, networking, and positive thinking.

What is PIP like?

Even higher standards are expected of each PIP Cadet as are expected of the Phase 1 and CCLD Cadets. PIP Cadets are expected to arrive standing tall and looking sharp on day one to pick up right where they left off after Phase 2. The atmosphere at the camp for a PIP Cadet will not be as rigid as Phase 1 and CCLD. We presume that each PIP Cadet will have the ability to easily conduct his or herself with the utmost honor and self-discipline. You will eat with all other phases of cadets. You will have many responsibilities in leading the underclassmen in PT, drill, and other activities as you will be heavily relied upon as a junior counselor. You will attend some classes of Phase 1 and CCLD to observe and provide feedback to staff. You will be expected to constantly provide feedback in relation to all aspects of Phase 1 and CCLD as well as PIP for improving the programs. You will have self-improvement classes as well as brainstorming meetings regarding future Troop D Camp Cadet fundraising and recruiting. Throughout the year, you can conduct the fundraising and recruiting programs that PIP had developed.

Besides multiple Camp Cadets, another camp was formed called Commissioner's Honor Camp. Corporal Joe Nolte explains, "In the fall of 1997, then Commissioner Colonel Paul J. Evanko pitched his idea of an all-star type of Camp Cadet program to the annual meeting of Community Service Officers (CSO) at the Academy.

Corporal Joseph P. Nolte

"Colonel Evanko wanted to have the best two cadets from each local Camp Cadet program to attend this new annual endeavor. He said he didn't know how it was to be funded, who was going to run it or how the participants would be selected, but he wanted it done. Because of the geographical location of the Pennsylvania State Police Academy, I was most vocal about not infringing on South Central Camp Cadet's fundraising efforts. Because of this (and the fact they probably didn't want the additional workload), individuals in attendance suggested that I run the program.

"I took the assignment with open arms. In 1998, we gathered some of the key people from around the Commonwealth (Trooper Albert R. Vish, Butler County; Ms. Nancy Bard, RN, Butler County; Sgt. Art Hershey, Bedford County; Ms. Julia Montgomery, Bedford County; Mr. Dave Dubner, Montgomery County) to trade and share ideas about what should be included in the program. We applied for and received 501(c)(3) status, and the program was officially established in 1998. The actual first camp was held at the academy in the summer of 1999. It has been continuous since that date.

"From its inception, this was created to show the kids a more in-depth working knowledge of state government, particularly the Pennsylvania State Police. Many of the local Camp Cadet programs rely on municipal and other law enforcement agencies to accomplish their goals. The Commissioner's Honor Camp Board of Directors decided that this program should be staffed solely by Pennsylvania State Police personnel and all programming conducted by same. Its board of directors are Corporal Joseph P. Nolte (1998–2013), Sergeant Robert Bemis (2013–2016), and Corporal Morgan Crummy (2016–present)."

Corporal Joseph P. Nolte, born and raised in Pittsburgh, Pennsylvania, enlisted in the Pennsylvania State Police in February 1992, married to wife Lori Nolte since October 10, 1992, and retired January 2015 currently living in York, Pennsylvania.

He received his bachelor of science degree in 1988 from Slippery Rock University, worked for the United States National Park Service in Virginia and West Virginia (1988–1990), then Pennsylvania State Police, Bureau of Liquor Control Enforcement, Punxsutawney District Office as liquor control enforcement officer. In July 1992, he was assigned as a trooper to Troop H York Patrol then in January

1994 became the Troop H Harrisburg, community service officer (CSO) and program coordinator and director of South Central Camp Cadet, Inc.

In December 2002, Joe was transferred to the PSP Academy as the statewide coordinator, including oversight of Camp Cadet. Among his accomplishments included writing a manual on Camp Cadet to include all aspects of forming a 501(c)(3) nonprofit program, fundraising, sample itineraries/lesson plans, meals, and contacts for merchandise to use as fundraisers. Transferred in 2007, to the video production section at the academy, Joe became more involved in Pennsylvania State Police Cadet training, online training, and training video production.

In July 2008, promotion to corporal was followed by a transfer to the executive service section of the Governor's Protection Detail December 2011, serving as supervisor during the administrations of the Honorable Tom Corbett and his successor, Tom Wolf, until retirement on January 30, 2015. Joe remains active in the South Central Camp Cadet program serving as the president of the board of directors.

OUTSIDE OF
PENNSYLVANIA

Mentoring America's Youth author Evan K. Slaughenhoupt Jr., when a teenager, wanted to become a state policeman and joined an Explorer Club sponsored by Troop D and led by Sergeant Hartung then later led by Trooper Robert W. Price. About once a month, meetings were held in the basement of the police barracks. The Explorer Club provided patches to wear that were sewn onto dark blue light wear jackets. One highlight occurred when the explorers served as ushers during a fundraising basketball game at Butler High School between the state police and the Pittsburgh Steelers football team.

Another highlight occurred when guest speakers visited the monthly meetings. One memorable event included a guest speaker named Trooper Albert R. Vish. His personality shined immediately as he spoke, jokingly telling the explorers to pay attention. It is said that it's not so much what somebody says that is caused to be remembered but that people will remember how they felt. So true as from then, Al became a lifelong role model, mentor, and friend.

The explorers would learn about plans for the upcoming first-ever Camp Cadet. Being one year too old to be a camper, I did attend that graduation ceremony. The following year right after high school graduation in 1971, I was accepted to serve as a counselor for the second Camp Cadet. Throughout service in the Air Force and for a few years after that, a combination of Permissive Temporary Duty (TDY) or leave/vacation time afforded further counseling opportunities at Camp Cadet. It became an honor and privilege.

Following military service and during years in the department of defense overseas assignments caused for a parting from Camp Cadet after the 1978 camp, except for an opportunity one year in 1987. Life took its various paths and Camp Cadet became a distant fond memory.

Retirement for me from federal service followed by employment for a defense contractor provided an opportunity to get more involved in local community affairs. Eventually joining and becoming president of a community association, an opportunity arose to seek political elected office. In short, I was elected in 2010 and reelected in 2014, as a Calvert County, Maryland, County Commissioner serving two terms before retiring in 2018.

Calvert County, Maryland, has four public high schools Northern, Huntingtown, Calvert, and Patuxent High Schools. The first week of June brings the graduations that occur at an equestrian center in nearby Prince Georges County. Typically, two schools graduate on Wednesday and the other two on Thursday. Each day between the two graduations, a dinner is provided for guests such as county commissioners, board of education, and law enforcement who also provide security during the graduation.

During an otherwise 2012 uneventful graduation dinner, I decided to sit with the Calvert County deputies, sheriff, and state troopers. Being the only civilian at the table was like being a thumb as the conversation was very much law enforcement type chatter. At one point, a deputy or the sheriff asked the state troopers if they were going to have another Camp COPS that year. As the response included some of the planning details, I responded, "That sounds like Camp Cadet to me."

As if rehearsed, each of the law enforcement individuals at the table turned to look in amazement with one asking, "How do you know about Camp Cadet?"

"Easy, my good friend Al Vish created Camp Cadet and I was a counselor there for several years."

The Maryland State Troopers explained that one of theirs, Trooper Bonnie Morris learned of Camp Cadet and brought the concept to Calvert County. One observation where the camps differ: the

Maryland camp has the parents drop off and pick up campers each day (not overnighting). Camp Cadet received the youth on Sunday, and the parents did not typically see them until after hearing the cadets march into the ceremony the following Saturday.

Calvert County, Maryland, County Commissioner
Evan K. Slaughenhoupt Jr.

Taking the opportunity to reach out and make a connection, within days, Al Vish and wife Mickey were making plans to visit Calvert County for a couple of days while traveling to visit family in Richmond, Virginia. Al and Mickey did visit, toured the county, and sampled local restaurants and, at 3:00 p.m., on July 30, 2012, attended the Sixteenth Annual Camp COPS Graduation Ceremony. Following opening remarks by Maryland State Police Barrack "U" Commander Lt. Randy Stephens and the Pledge of Allegiance, two special guests were invited to address the audience. As commissioner, provided background about Camp Cadet, how honored everyone was to hear from and then introduced the creator of Camp Cadet.

Pictured moments before ceremony

Al also received a proclamation signed by all five Calvert County Commissioners and a Calvert County flag.

Al Vish addressed the audience as only he could with his remarks to the campers beginning with, "You are valued." Later, in recognition of honor among brothers, the Maryland State Police provided a Maryland State Police patch to Commissioner Slaughenhoupt who mailed it to Al.

Maryland State Police Emblem

Pennsylvania State Police Emblems
1959–1987

Pennsylvania State Police Emblem
1987–Present

Envision how two individuals meeting in 1970, in Pennsylvania, involved in a unique program such as Camp Cadet take their own paths, and then forty-two years later rejoin in Maryland participating in graduation program formed directly from the model set by Camp Cadet. The only thing that makes sense is divine intervention. That once in a lifetime unrepeatable event, something remarkable occurred to permit this full circle in life between Trooper Albert R. Vish and me. *Mentoring America's Youth* resulted hopeful of advancing the details of this unique program potentially benefiting many throughout America by its publication. The history of Camp Cadet is very much like a partial biography of Trooper Albert R. Vish. The two are much intertwined, one and the same. Trying to balance between the two keeping focus on the camp program was a challenge. Hopefully, the reader will agree with the balance sought.

Outside of Pennsylvania and the previously mentioned Maryland Camp COPS, at least one camp exists in Florida and has a presence on Facebook that says, "The purpose of Northeast Florida Camp Cadet, Inc. is to provide today's youth with the tools necessary to overcome challenges, instill strict discipline and bestow confidence and leadership abilities.

"Camp Cadet is a tuition-free, one-week event, staffed by local police and sheriff's departments from Clay, Duval, Bradford, and Nassau counties. The police officers and deputies of these counties serve as counselors and instructors. The program is designed to give boys and girls, ages twelve through fifteen, a better understanding of law enforcement activities while living in an atmosphere similar to a police training academy. It is held at Northfork Leadership Center in Middleburg, Florida. Heavy emphasis is placed on leadership by improving self-discipline, building self-esteem and confidence through teamwork and making new friends.

"Camp Cadet was originally formed in 1970 by Trooper Albert R. Vish of the Pennsylvania State Police. Trooper Vish, along with Troopers John Prandy (deceased) and Robert Price (deceased), was instrumental in establishing the first Camp Cadet in Butler County. Since 1970, Camp Cadet programs have been established in approximately thirty other counties in Pennsylvania. Officer Kimberly Robinson of the Green Cove Springs Police Department was formerly a police officer in Pennsylvania. Officer Robinson was the first president of the Allegheny County Camp Cadet. After assisting Trooper Robin Mungo in Allegheny County Pennsylvania, she decided to start a Camp Cadet in Northeast Florida."

Camp Cadet is alive today and continues to grow keeping the initial goals flourishing throughout America. The following pages may not capture every camp but is an indicator just how the original idea by Trooper Albert R. Vish has matured.

Troop	County, State	Website/Reference	Comments
	Clay Duval Bradford Nassau Florida	https://www.flcampcadet.com/	Held at Northfork Leadership Center in Middleburg Florida.
Troop	County, State	Website/Reference	Comments
G U	Carroll Calvert Maryland	http://www.mdsp. org/Document%20 Downloads/2013%20 Annual%20Report%20FINAL. pdf	Camp COPS (Courage to be Outstanding with Pride and Self-Confidence)
	Pennsylvania	https://www.psp.pa.gov/public-safety/Pages/Camp-Cadet-Summer-Program.aspx	
A	Somerset Westmoreland	http://www. westmorelandcampcadet.org/ HomeComponent	
	Indiana	http://www. indianacountycampcadet.org/ home.html	Camp Seph Mack, BSA in Penn Run, Pennsylvania
	Cambria	https://www. cambriacountycampcadet.org/	
B	Allegheny Fayette Greene Washington	http://www. alleghenycountycampcadet.org/	Camp Guvasuta in Sharpsburg, just outside of Pittsburgh
Troop	County, State	Website/Reference	Comments
C	Clarion Jefferson, Clearfield Elk Forest McKean Northern Indiana	Trooper Bruce A. Morris in Ridgeway at 814-772-2399 or bmorris@pa.gov	

Troop	County, State	Website/Reference	Comments
D	Armstrong Beaver Butler Lawrence Mercer	http://troopdcampcadet.org/	Original
E	Crawford Erie Venango Warren	https://www.pacampcadet.com/	Allegheny College
F	Cameron Clinton Lycoming Montour Northumberland Potter Snyder Tioga Union	https://www.psp.pa.gov/ troop%20directory/Pages/ Troop-F.aspx https://www.lyco.org/ Elected-Officials/Sheriff/ Camp-Cadet	Split between Northern and Southern Tier Camp Cadets
G	Bedford Blair Centre Fulton Huntingdon Juniata Mifflin	https://www. campcadetbedfordco.org/ https://sites.google.com/site/ centrecountylawenforcementinc/	Centre County camp is at Camp Blue Diamond located at 4013 Blue Diamond Dr. Petersburg, Pennsylvania 16669
Troop	County, State	Website/Reference	Comments
H	Adams Cumberland Dauphin Franklin Perry	https://southcentralcampcadet. org/	
J	Chester	http://www.cccampcadet.org/	
	Lancaster	http:// campcadetoflancastercounty. com/	
	York	https://southcentralcampcadet. org/	